Changing Perceptions of Aging and the Aged

Dena Shenk, PhD, is Professor, Department of Sociology, Anthropology, and Social Work, and Coordinator, Gerontology Program, University of North Carolina at Charlotte. She now prefers to think of herself as an anthropological gerontologist. "It was an evolution," she says. "In high school and college I was fascinated with the way of understanding people, societies, and cultures that anthropology provided. I've used it ever since as an orientation for making sense of the world—personally and professionally." After receiving her Bachelor's degree in anthropology from the State University of New York, she decided that her focus would be on aging. At the University of Massachusetts, where she did her doctoral work, there was a good anthropology program and individual gerontology courses, but no formal program. So, Shenk says, she basically developed her own course of study. "That was quite common for those of us interested in aging at the time. In the mid 70's an association for anthropology and gerontology was formed, and we started coming together, realizing there was more of us out there. We were all interested in how people age in other societies as well as our own."

Since that time, Shenk has been a major force in the development of the field of anthropology and aging, publishing widely and establishing an interdisciplinary master's program in gerontology at St. Cloud State University. At the University of North Carolina at Charlotte, she is developing the undergraduate and planning the graduate program in gerontology.

She is particularly well known for her application of anthropological gerontology to the study of populations in the United States, especially ethnic groups and, most recently, the social networks of rural older women.

W. Andrew Achenbaum, PhD, is Professor of History and Deputy Director, Institute of Gerontology, University of Michigan, Ann Arbor. He received his Bachelor's degree in American studies from Amherst, a Master's in American civilization from the University of Pennsylvania, and his doctorate in history from the University of Michigan, because its program could accommode his interest in aging.

Since then, Achenbaum has distinguished himself in his chosen realm, through teaching, research, and administration, and is recognized as one of the most creative thinkers in the field. He is the author of acclaimed books and articles that range from historical studies of aging in America to critical exploration of such matters as research on the biology of aging, based on a historical view. "It's wonderful for a historian to be able to apply history to nitty-gritty issues," Achenbaum says. "Perspective is what history can provide. Some things don't change, and some things do."

Dr. Achenbaum is currently completing a history of gerontology. He also plans a biography of wise Twentieth-Century people and is the co-editor of *Voices and Visions of Aging: Toward a Critical Gerontology*, published by Springer Publishing Company in 1993.

Changing Perceptions of Aging and the Aged

Dena Shenk, PhD
W. Andrew Achenbaum, PhD
Editors   WITHDRAWN

Originally published as the Spring/Summer 1993 issue of
Generations, Journal of the American Society on Aging,
Mary Johnson, Editor

Springer Publishing Company
New York

Cover and interior design by Holly A. Block
Production Editor: Pam Ritzer

Springer Publishing Company, Inc.
536 Broadway
New York, NY 10012

94 95 96 97 98 / 5 4 3 2 1

Library of Congress Cataloging-in-Publication Data

Changing perceptions of aging and the aged / Dena Shenk, W. Andrew
Achenbaum, editors.
    p.   cm.
 Originally issued as v. 17, no. 2 of *Generations,* the quarterly
journal of the American Society on Aging.
    Includes bibliographical references and index.
    ISBN 0-8261-8420-0
    1. Aged in popular culture. 2. Ageism. I. Shenk, Dena.
II. Achenbaum. W. Andrew.
HQ1061.C377 1994
305.26—dc20

Printed in the United States of America

CONTENTS

v

Contents

CONTRIBUTORS

Robert N. Butler, MD, is a Brookdale Professor of Geriatrics and Adult Development, and Chairman, Department of Geriatrics and Adult Development, Mount Sinai School of Medicine, New York.

Iris Carlton-LaNey, PhD, is Associate Professor, Department of Sociology, Anthropology, and Social Work, University of North Carolina at Charlotte.

Leonard Cirillo, PhD, is Associate Professor of Psychology, Frances L. Hiatt School of Psychology, Clark University, Worcester, MA.

Douglas E. Crews, PhD, is Assistant Professor of Anthropology and Preventive Medicine, Ohio State University, Columbus.

Judith de Luce, PhD, is Professor, Department of Classics, and Fellow, Scripps Gerontology Center, Miami University, Oxford, OH.

Carole Haber, PhD, received her PhD from the Department of American Civilization at the University of Pennsylvania and is currently a Professor of History, University of North Carolina at Charlotte.

Robert B. Hudson, PhD, is Professor of Social Welfare Policy, School of Social Work, Boston University.

Sharon R. Kaufman, PhD, is Associate Research Anthropologist affiliated with the Institute for Health and Aging and the Medical Anthropology Program, University of California, San Francisco.

Mel Kimble, PhD, is Professor of Pastoral Theology and Director, Program in Aging, Luther Northwestern Theological Seminary, St. Paul, MN.

Joanne Leonard is a Professor, School of Art and Associate, American Culture Program, University of Michigan, Ann Arbor.

Graham D. Rowles, PhD, is Professor of Geography and Behavioral Science and Associate Director of the Sanders-Brown Center on Aging, University of Kentucky, Lexington.

Andrea Sankar, PhD, is Associate Professor and Director of the Medical Anthropology Program, Wayne State University, Detroit, MI.

Ron Schmid is a professional photographer in St. Cloud, MN.

Jay Sokolovsky, PhD, is Professor of Anthropology, University of Maryland, Baltimore Country.

Maria D. Vesperi, PhD, is a Cultural Anthropologist and a member of the *St. Petersburg Times* editorial board. In the fall, she will join the faculty of New College of the University of South Florida, Sarasota.

Contributors

Steven Weiland is Professor of Higher Education at Michigan State University, East Lansing.

Kathleen Woodward, PhD, is Professor, Department of English and Comparative Literature, University of Wisconsin, Milwaukee.

Robert E. Yahnke, PhD, is Professor of Literature and Film at the General College, University of Minnesota, Minneapolis.

Introduction

When we accepted the task of editing a book based on a special issue of *Generations* on images and perceptions of age and aging, we were attracted both by the challenge of the project and the importance and timeliness of the topic. Images and perceptions of age and aging are important concepts for those of us who work with the aged and seek to understand the aging process.

Perceptions of the aged, like other broadly defined groups of people (e.g., politicians or college students), are generally characterized by a range of stereotyped images. American college students in class exercises typically characterize "old people" in terms of both negative and positive stereotypes. The negative stereotypes include primarily physical traits like slow, feeble, and gray-haired, and personality traits like cranky and repetitive. College students' positive stereotypes of "old people" tend to focus on personality traits like sweet and caring. These positive traits are typically passive, viewing the elderly as "pleasant" and "storytellers."

When instructed to describe a particular older person, students generally write positive portrayals, often about healthy, active older individuals. They tend, however, to think of these older individuals as exceptions to the rule, rather than changing the "rule" or their views of older adults. Each of us knows active, healthy individuals—some are older and some are younger and middle-aged. Similarly, we can each describe a cranky, rigid individual—and in reality this generally has nothing to do with the person's age. A person can be cranky and rigid at 21 as well as active and open-minded at 81. Yet stereotypes of older adults abound and lead people of all ages to approach aging and the aged as if these stereotyped images were true. This situation demonstrates the potential harm of stereotyped images. It also suggests the promise that we see in understanding the role that images and perceptions of age and aging play and the nature of these images.

Images of age and aging matter greatly because postwar Americans more and more think generically in terms of images and respond to their subtle cues. According to the historian and former Librarian of Congress Daniel Boorstin (1977, p. 185), images have become pseudo-ideals. They are "synthetic, believable, passive, vivid, simplified and ambiguous." By "synthetic," Boorstin means that images of reality are crafted, or to use contemporary academic parlance, carefully "constructed." Hence trademarks like IBM are so well established that mere letters of the alphabet have come to draw together ideas about communication, corporate life, and the future.

Images are most effective when they enable viewers to imagine depths of insight and meanings that are not "really" embodied in the artifact but which, nonetheless, seem artfully straightforward as soon as they are decoded by the mind's eye. Most advertisements use words sparingly because they are designed to invoke subliminal messages. Their appealing re-presentation of reality induces customers to purchase goods. Paradoxically, ad agencies' images actively work to be passive. They conform to the commonplace in a shrewdly calculating manner. So we no longer buy cough drops from the bearded Smith Brothers or remember the breed of the dog listening to "His Master's Voice" on that phonograph, but we do not quickly forget those images. Vivid images have staying power in large part because they are so ambiguous. Even when they become obsolete, they maintain a niche in popular culture, serving as a caricature of the world and worldviews that once sustained them.

Much that Daniel Boorstin says about images in general applies to prevailing images of older Americans. Canes and gray hair have been icons of age since ancient times. With enough makeup a 20-year-old model can look "mature," but even Lauren Hutton's exquisite face is more likely to be found on the cover of *Lear's* than *Vogue*. In advertisements as well as sitcoms, older characters still tend to fit the stereotypes, although some of the stereotypes are now positive. But with gains in adult life expectancy and, lately, an ugly turn in the politics of aging, among other things, older people are no longer "marginalized" in our fields of vision.

Provocative images of "greedy geezers" frittering away their (grand)children's inheritance in self-indulgent excesses have recently illustrated media cover stories. Never mind that the graphics grossly ignore profound differences in the economic circumstance among elders. These graphics sell magazines. Especially now, when our understanding of what it means to grow older is in flux, and when it seems quite likely that a new generation of officials in Washington will rethink old-age politics, the very ambiguities that inhere in our images of late life may hamper as much as they facilitate efforts to take a detached view of the status of Older America. Taking a fresh look with a critical eye at images of age, in other words, is an immensely practical task.

In the absence of sustained academic inquiry into the contours and dynamics of images of (old) age (Achenbaum, forthcoming; Cole, Van Tassel and Kastenbaum, 1992, and Polisar et al., 1988), those who shape American popular and elite culture have nonetheless been transforming its prevailing perceptions. There is little empirical evidence to sustain the notion that future conflicts over justice, wealth, and power in U.S. society will inexorably divide over questions of "generational equity." Age is an important marker of social, economic, and political status in America. Yet historically, race, gender, and class have divided the American people in more appalling ways. These three factors doubtless will remain more influential than age in social interactions for decades to come.

But the rhetorical power embodied by the image of "generational equity" does not need scientific data to bolster and sustain its impact on popular attitudes and stereotypes. Word-pictures used to illustrate the "burden" of aging underscore as they feed upon people's fears (Warnes, forthcoming). Images entice us to pity the young men and women struggling to the top of the hill bent under the dead weight of an older generation. Cartoons of the see-saw that will never get off the ground warn us about what we face in the future unless the cost of caring for the aged is reduced. Such images oversimplify complex relationships, stressing the weakness and obsolescence of the old. (Those who remember Kipling's "White Man's Burden" may even see analogies between racism and ageism.) The images do not focus on mutual reciprocity, or what precisely is entailed in the duties of caregivers. And what is not focused on or stated often is ignored.

As a new administration defines its priorities in Washington, images of old age, for better and for worse, are bound to affect new directions in federal policies. How future programs will unfold is unclear. None of the major candidates talked much about older people, and references to Social Security intentionally were kept vague. Everybody wants better health insurance programs, but how long-term care or catastrophic coverage would fit into the package is left to the public's imagination.

Animating any political calculations or policy reform will be images of the elderly. What proportion of the elderly are "needy"? Are the generations of Americans who came of age since Watergate simply selfish and avaricious as some neoconservative Boomer commentators would have us believe? Older people are typically portrayed as sicker than younger people, but is Alzheimer's the fate that awaits all who live (too) long? Are the old-old capable of contributing anything meaningful to society? Is there an image that appropriately accompanies Daniel Callahan's notion of Setting Limits (1987)? Do such questions indicate that the aged as a group, as Robert Binstock (1983) suggested, deservedly are becoming "scapegoats" for those who want to reduce the budget deficit as painlessly as possible?

The chapters in this issue focus on a broad array of images of aging in a variety of cultural and historical contexts. The range of perceptions of age and aging can be broadly characterized into three main types. First are the negative views of aging, which often focus on physical decline. These negative images form the basis for "ageism," the term originally coined by Robert Butler and reexamined by him in Chapter 15. Among others, the chapters by Judith de Luce and Kathleen Woodward focus on these negative portrayals of age. A second view of age focuses on the positive aspects of aging, characterizing old age as a period of wisdom and maturity. These positive images of aging often accompany the quest for "successful aging." Iris Carlton-LaNey's portrayal of rural Southern women represents such a positive image of age. A third image of age and aging can be described by the phrase "old people are people." This conception of old people as people was spelled out by Jennie Keith in her book *Old People as People* (1982). This image of age and the aged leads to consideration of the differences between individuals and a focus on the nature of the aging experience for specific individuals. Several chapters in this book reflect this approach, including those by Sharon Kaufman and Graham Rowles and the photoessay by Dena Shenk and Ron Schmid.

"Images and perceptions of age" is a big topic, and that is the challenge of this book. The editors knew at the outset that they could not deal with all of the important themes in these pages. Accordingly, with the able assistance of *Generations*'s editorial board, the ASA staff, and colleagues, we made two decisions that guided our choice of chapters and selection of authors.

First, we realized that not all pertinent images of age carry over to all segments of society in similar ways. Most images, in fact, operate at different levels of cognition and in varying domains. Some are very personal and operate at the individual level: They reflect the ways we think about our aging bodies and own aging experience. Other images are institution-specific: Professional conventions, such as the age-graded rites of the academic tribe, dictate how one expresses images of writing or teaching, or in Hollywood, how the elderly are best portrayed on-screen. Still others are cultural: Such images not only encapsulate prevailing societal definitions of age-specific norms and expectations, but they also are shaped by current economic trends, political events, and social tastes.

At every level, images and perceptions of age are also powerfully influenced by other images. All old people are not alike. The heterogeneity of old people bespeaks differences in race, gender, class, educational status, geographic location, and religious thoughts. Because we began our discussion of the themes of this book with the notion that we wanted to highlight the diversity of old-age images, we eschewed a comprehensive approach to the subject matter. We selected case studies that focused on major image-makers and images of age that were constructed from different perspectives.

Second, we recruited authors whose previous writings about perceptions of age and aging impressed us. Rather than ask our contributors to necessarily give us more of the same, however, we invited some of them to critically answer two sets of questions. On the one hand, we asked them to reconsider their earlier work, and then tell us what has changed about images of age since they first dealt with the topic. Are there new images? Are they more positive or negative or simply ambiguous in different ways? Were old ideas reworked into new stereotypes? Is gender/race/class more pivotal in discriminating among images of the elderly? On the other hand, authors were invited to consider the effects of their own experiences of growing older on their perceptions and interpretations of images of aging. Do they pay more attention to the materials in the shadows? Are they less (or more!) willing to equivocate? Do they view images of age with a sharper eye? By allowing authors to be self-reflexive, we hoped to introduce a more critical stance toward their subtopic. Without belaboring this theme, we wanted authors to re-view images of old age, which we suspect are in flux because they are themselves re-presentations of reality.

This volume is organized into three parts, with an underlying theme of how perceptions of age and aging change over time. The first part includes chapters focusing on the personal aging experience and perceptions of age on the individual level. Sharon Kaufman's reflections on her concept of the "ageless self" describes the development of this notion of agelessness. Her emphasis is on older persons' interpretations of meaningful issues in late life. The chapters by Steve Weiland and Kathleen Woodward explore the specific cases of Erik Erikson and Simone de Beauvoir. Woodward reconsiders the negative portrayal of aging in *Coming of Age* in terms of de Beauvoir's own life as an older woman. Weiland offers a reconsideration of Erikson's career, analyzing how Erikson himself has sought to move beyond his own developmental theory. In his vignette, Mel Kimble explores how the spiritual dimension has been manifested through his personal journey of aging.

The second part focuses on varieties in the perceptions of age and aging, including examples from various cultures and subcultures over time. Jay Sokolovsky's global perspective on perceptions and images of aging cross-culturally provides an overview. He examines how cultural variation relates to created images of aging and, particularly, cultural images of nonfunctional elders. Several of the chapters offer analyses of perceptions of aging within the United States. These include Iris Carlton-LaNey's moving discussion of aging Southern black women, Carole Haber's historical perspective on the fear of old-age impoverishment in the early twentieth century, and Achenbaum's reconsideration of his study of images of old age between 1790 and 1970. Andrea Sankar presents a rethinking of images of home death in relation to the elderly patient. The dynamic nature of cultural images of "aging in place" is explored by Graham Rowles, who critiques this current focus in light of contemporary realities and new forms of affiliation with place in our country. Doug Crews presents the concept of "cultural lag" to explain how perceptions of age and aging can be "out of synch" because of changes and transitions within a society. Judith de Luce discusses perceptions of age and aging in ancient Greece and Rome, examining whether ageism existed. The final chapter in this part is a photographic essay by Dena Shenk and Ron Schmid that presents their ongoing work with photographic images of aging women.

The third part includes chapters focusing on institutional and literary responses to images and perceptions of age and aging. Robert Butler's reconsideration of the concept of "ageism" finds that ageism still exists. He discusses current manifestations and recommends a variety of interventions for dispelling ageism. Robert Hudson's reconsideration of his 1978 article on the "graying" of the federal budget recognizes the role of class and generation in current aging-related politics. Literary and media images of age and aging are discussed by Robert Yahnke, Maria Vesperi, and Leonard Cirillo. Yahnke provides an overview of representations of aging in contemporary American literature, identifying three key themes. From the intriguing dual perspective of a print journalist who is also a cultural anthropologist, Maria Vesperi analyzes the content and layout of news stories about the elderly, identifying four broad formats. Finally, Cirillo explores the verbal imagery about aging and the aged used in news magazines.

DENA SHENK
W. ANDREW ACHENBAUM

References

Achenbaum, W. A., forthcoming. "Images of Old Age and Aging: The State of the Art," to appear in *Reviews in Clinical Gerontology*.

Binstock, R. H., 1983. "The Aged as Scapegoat." *Gerontologist* 23: 136–43.

Boorstin, D., 1977. *The Image*. New York: Atheneum.

Callahan, D., 1987. *Setting Limits*. New York: Simon & Schuster.

Cole, T. R., Van Tassel, D. D., and Kastenbaum, R., eds., 1992. *Handbook of*

Introduction

Humanities and Aging. New York: Springer Publishing Co.

Keith, J., *1982. Old People as People: Social and Cultural Influences on Aging and Old Age.* Boston: Little, Brown.

Polisar, D., et al., 1988. *Where Do We Come From? What Are We? Where Are We Going?* Washington, D.C.: Gerontological Society of America.

Warnes, A. M., forthcoming. "Elderly People and the Burdens of Burden," to appear in *Ageing and Society.*

PART ONE

Personal and Individual Perceptions

Not Losing Her Memory

Images of Family in Photography, Words, and Collage

Joanne Leonard

S tand over there so I can see how I look" is something either I or my twin sister is supposed to have once said as a child. I am a twin. Thinking in plurals has not been foreign to me. The idea that any story about self is really a story about multiple selves comes easily to me. It follows that the distinctions between autobiography and biography are not always clear, and I have exploited the unclear boundaries of these two forms of relating life stories in "Not Losing Her Memory," a photocollage project from which the images on these pages are taken.

My grandmother died when I was only two, and I had no conscious memory of her. Two framed and stunning Edward Weston photographs of her have been in our home all of my life and have become, for me, emblematic visions of her. These two portraits, from among the Weston portraits commissioned, figure repeatedly in my photocollage series. My discovery that the two photographs I owned were part of a cache of 27 negatives by Weston of my grandmother (the negatives are now housed at the University of Arizona's Center for Creative Photography) launched me on this project, which began with a trip to Los Angeles. With my twin sister, Elly, and my daughter, Julia, I visited my grandmother's former Los Angeles home and, with the homeowner's permission, photographed Elly and Julia where Ida (Peg) G.

3

PERSONAL AND INDIVIDUAL PERCEPTIONS

Batelle, my grandmother, had stood before Weston's camera.

My sister and I used to beg my mother to say which twin was which in our early family photographs. My mother would usually satisfy us with an answer after only a slight pause. From my adult vantage, I suppose she sometimes invented her answer (we were really difficult to tell

Conversation (collage incorporates photo by the author of her mother, early 1970s, at left, and photo by Edward Weston of the author's grandmother, 1934, at right). In my collages I stage conversation between my mother and grandmother. I give them a new space where they can talk across the generations, across the distance of things that were never said, across the misunderstandings, regrets, deaths, memory losses.

apart as infants), and this thought suggests the inevitable fictive aspects of biography and autobiography. Through collage, photography, and text, I have relished the family resemblances and "twinning" amid and across generations. In my work I have blurred the distinction between our (my twin sister's and my own) memory and my mother's, and between biography, autobiography, memory, invention, and history.

My autobiographic work has been consciously fragmentary, not only because autobiographic work is necessarily so, but also as a deliberate strategy. I have used fragmenting, layering, overlapping, and repeating of images and text as signs for the imprecise process of remembering and for memory loss, the tragic loss of self. My mother died toward the end of the time I was creating these works, but even before

Resemblance of Things Past (collage incorporates photos by the author and lower far left, Edward Weston). An adopted person or someone estranged from family resemblances that I have taken throughout the evolution of my project. Such a person's way of "imaging" family and memory would necessarily take forms different from my own.

Four Generations, One Absent. (collage incorporates photos by the author and, far right, Edward Weston). When I began to fit the Weston images and my own photographs together in collage, I frequently wove in bits of text. Here are four generations or, rather, three—with words in the place where my mother should be. Setting it up as I have, with Julia, my daughter far to the left, looking back, surveying those who came before, I have created space for longing. In the space where my mother's picture might have been, I wrote the following: "My mother is missing, not just missing here, on paper by actually. She has no memory, and that is an absence beyond any."

her death, while she lived in the grip of Alzheimer's disease, she was dead as a "speaking subject." We, her daughters, became her voice, her memory, and have further blurred the boundaries between memory and imaginations as we have worked to use our visual forms to comment and respond. In some of the works where my mother is not actually depicted, there is an empty space where she might belong. In her place are my

Devastation (collage incorporates photo by the author). One of my saddest moments was seeing the graphic evidence of my mother's loss of language. My remarkable mother, a brilliant and pioneering child psychoanalyst who had been trained by members of Freud's inner circle, now wrote my sister a note that we could not read. My mother's mind had come to resemble the crossed wires downed in a hurricane, and it was difficult for her to undertake a task as simple as recognizing and drinking a glass of milk.

7

words, "My mother is missing, not just missing here, on paper, but actually. She has no memory, and that is an absence beyond any."

In creating this work, I have touched somewhat on issues of sexuality, gender, race, class, and ethnicity. By concentrating on the women in my family, I have tried to represent my self/selves among others, as well as to suggest the untold and untellable among the family stories and histories.

Study: Stories from My Mother's Garden (collage incorporates photo by the author). Carolyn Heilbrun's words became important to me as a kind of summing up. In her book Writing a Woman's Life (Norton, 1988), she wrote the following, which I copied into my work: "We tell ourselves stories of our past, make fictions or stories of it, and these narratives become the past, the only part or our lives that is not submerged."

Acknowledgments

Much of this material first appeared in Passages North (Vol. 13[3]) and is reprinted here with permission.

Reflections on 'The Ageless Self'

Sharon R. Kaufman

T here can be no doubt that gerontology's vision of aging and the aged has changed markedly in the last decade, influenced by both a growing awareness of the varieties of the aging experience around the world and the impact of the "soft" social sciences and humanities on our hybrid discipline. When I entered the field in 1975, gerontology modeled itself as a largely scientific field, based for the most part on academic traditions in developmental psychology, sociology, and biology. Gerontology's theories about old people and the aging process reflected the dominant patterns and paradigms of research in those parent disciplines and produced a notion of aging based on quantitative research methods, the gathering of "hard" and "objective" data, and the exploration of certain constructs that were of interest to many in the field. Thus gerontologists devised such concepts as "life satisfaction" and "morale" and formulated theories such as "disengagement," "activity," and "continuity" in attempts to understand and predict psychosocial dimensions of the aging process. They also studied loss and decline—physiological, psychosocial, economic, political—and the relationship of those losses to chronological age in order to identify and understand the problems and needs of a growing elderly population. Those constructs and theories were born of an era when "value-free empiricism" and instrumental research were assumed to be an appropriate way to ask and answer questions about human behavior and adult development.

11

PERSONAL AND INDIVIDUAL PERCEPTIONS

My study of identity development and sources of meaning in late life emerged from my awareness of the limits of experimental science as applied to the study of aging (Kaufman, 1986). I was acutely aware of the fact that the voices of individual old people were de-emphasized or lost in the conduct of that type of research. I wanted to look at the meaning of aging to elderly people themselves, as it emerges in their personal reflections of growing old. That kind of inquiry requires the investigation of individual experience rather than the investigation of specific research variables. It requires looking at old people's accounts of the life course rather than employing theoretical concepts (such as trajectory or adaptation) to explain the nature of the aging process. My method was to ask old people to talk about their lives, with as little interference and guidance from me, the investigator/interviewer, as possible. My goal was to concentrate on the ways in which old people themselves interpreted their experience. I wanted to study aging through the expression of individual humanity; I wanted to bring the individual voice back into the research endeavor.

DEVELOPMENT OF 'THE AGELESS SELF'

To pursue my goals, I conducted anthropological fieldwork with people over the age of 70 in a variety of settings: nursing homes, retirement residences, senior centers, and retiree support groups. I met with them on a one-to-one basis for conversations and observed and participated with some of them in their daily rounds, with friends and family, in routine situations, and during periods of celebration, crisis, anxiety, and contentment.

In this way, I heard many older people talk about themselves, their pasts, and their concerns for the future. I observed that when they talk about who they are and how their lives have been, they do not speak of being old as meaningful in itself. That is, they do not relate to aging or chronological age as a category of experience or meaning. To the contrary, when old people talk about themselves, they express a sense of self that is ageless—an identity that maintains continuity despite the physical and social changes that come with old age. They may, in passing, describe themselves as "feeling old" in one context and "feeling young" or "not old" in another. This is always variable, and, in my experience, it is never emphasized. Old people do not perceive meaning in aging itself so much as they perceive meaning in being themselves in old age.

Thus, my initial research question about the meaning of aging evolved into an inquiry into identity, or the ageless self, and how it operates as a source of meaning in old age. In asking this question, my research focused not on a particular construct in gerontology and not on the changes that accompany old age. Rather, it explored what older people could tell me about their perceptions of growing and being old, their world view. It focused on how old people maintain a sense of continuity and meaning that helps them cope with change.

I found that the ageless self maintains continuity through a symbolic, creative process. The self draws meaning from the past, interpreting and re-creating it as a resource for being in the present. It also draws meaning from the structural and ideational aspects of the cultural context: social and educational background, family, work, values, ideals, and expectations. Identity is not frozen in a static moment of the past. Old people formulate and reformulate personal and cultural symbols of their past to create a meaningful, coherent sense of self, and in the process they create a viable present. In this way, the ageless self emerges: Its definition is ongoing, continuous, and creative.

SUBSEQUENT RESEARCH

My research in the last decade has focused on the illness experience in late life, especially the impact of chronic illness on notions of self and identity (Kaufman, 1988a, 1988b, 1988c).[1] In those phenomenological investigations, the concept of the ageless self has been confirmed. In illness, the self may be examined, redefined, and questioned, but it always remains the existential framework for dealing with the debilitating effects of disability and limitation. A self conceived as unbounded by time remains the central core through which illness is experienced, the mirror in which illness is reflected. Aging per se does not emerge as a salient feature of the illness experience or the recovery process.

For example, in in-depth, open-ended interviews with 64 stroke patients, three problems emerged as characterizing the poststroke experience: (1) the discontinuity of life patterns, (2) the failure to return to "normal," and (3) the redefined self.

Discontinuity

When people become patients, they discover that they cannot take the routine patterns of life for granted anymore. The familiar daily, weekly, and seasonal routines must be modified. Those routines become symbols of a self that used to be but is no longer. Depending on the level of disability, changes in life patterns may be either drastic or subtle. In either case, the person knows that life has changed and that he or she must actively and consciously make choices about behavior that previously had been assumed. People must plan their days and lives following a stroke—the long and short term—instead of just living them. Such highly conscious planning forces a confrontation between taken-for-granted past abilities and current circumstances until a meaningful sense of continuity can be created.

Not returning to "normal"

One may never return to previous conceptions of "normal." When research participants were asked, "Do you feel you have recovered from the stroke?" or "Do you feel your life is back to normal?" the answer was invariably "no." Even persons without visible disability gave this answer, for they believed that they were physically, emotionally, or cognitively different from their former selves, in spite of perfect performance in their rehabilitation therapy tasks.

Redefinition

Study subjects needed to learn whether they were the same as before the stroke. In the face of activities imposed by healthcare providers, curtailed daily routines, and physical losses, and with so many signs of normality and consistency gone, individuals searched for anchors of predictability. They sought to define and build links between the old self and the life ahead of them. That search and redefinition was their major task following a stroke. Its completion signified recovery, while achievement of discrete functional gains did not. Meeting the goals of rehabilitation therapists and other healthcare providers was thus of secondary importance and was viewed by most research participants as not particularly relevant to their own agenda: the need to show, through the ability to engage in former pursuits, that they were still the same kind of person they had always been (Becker, 1993; Becker & Kaufman, 1986; Kaufman, 1988a).

IMPLICATIONS FOR PRACTITIONERS

The integrative task of constantly creating the ageless self adds a cultural and biographical dimension to older persons as healthcare and social service recipients. Aging, and especially aging combined with ill-

14

ness, is more complex than a series of losses and attempts to adapt to them. It is rather an ongoing refitting and reformulating of images, symbols, and behaviors of the past into the circumstances of the present so that a sense of continuity emerges. Old people, even those who are quite isolated, continue to participate in society through whatever interactions they still retain, and more than this, old people continue to interpret their participation in the social world. As they cope with loss and change, they simultaneously create new meaning, building and creating the self in a dynamic, interactive way.

Regardless of whether or not older clients agree with practitioners' goals and treatment suggestions, they are existential beings, and as such, they hold onto a sense of self and sense of purpose that they generally refuse to have violated. It behooves practitioners to try to understand what that self is, so that their interventions fulfill, rather than conflict with, client priorities. Biographical knowledge of the client is thus essential in serving older adults. In order to implement a service plan, one must comprehend the meaning of illness or the meaning of certain behaviors to an individual. One needs to know who that person is, what matters to him or her, and the historical and social context of his or her decision making.

The notion of agelessness provides a framework for understanding the problems and needs that accompany aging. For old people do not think of themselves in a linear way—a succession of roles, or a trajectory of gains and losses. Nor do people think of themselves as purely "socialized" beings, learning, and then performing, a set of socially appropriate (or deviant) behaviors. Instead, people dynamically integrate a wide range of experience including values, family and educational backgrounds, work experience, and cultural ideals to construct a current identity. Decisions about what services to demand and what services to accept will depend on how perceptions of those services fit into their scheme of priorities—their ideas of what is important to them at that moment in time.

INTERPRETATION IN GERONTOLOGY

We know that chronological age alone explains nothing about human aging (Kastenbaum, 1987; Moody, 1988). Indeed, Neugarten (1977) long ago called age an "empty variable," stressing that it is the biological and social events associated with the passage of time, and not merely time itself, that have relevance for the study of identity development.

PERSONAL AND INDIVIDUAL PERCEPTIONS

I have found that while the biological and social changes that occur with time are relevant for the analysis of identity and aging, even more important are the ways in which these events are *interpreted* by older individuals—in relation to the passage of time and in relation to illness. Such interpretations have a great potential for explaining the process of change and continuity in late life.

Emphasis on older persons' interpretations of meaningful issues in late life suggests a reformulation of research agendas in gerontology. In such a reformulation, areas for investigation come not from gerontology's parent disciplines, but rather from old people themselves (Tornstam, 1992, p. 323). Tornstam (1992), Moody (1988), Neugarten (1984) and others have noted that our perceptions of aging and the aged have been shaped in large part by traditional, scientific paradigms in gerontology that (1) have a theoretical focus that is quite narrow, (2) reflect the dominant values of the researchers themselves rather than some objective truth, and (3) depict aging in predominantly negative terms. These scholars call for an opening up of the research enterprise to include humanistic (that is, nonexperimental), phenomenological, and other interpretive approaches.

A goal of phenomenological studies in the social sciences is to describe and clarify fundamental aspects of human experience (Frank, 1986): Phenomenology attends to the reality of experience. The term "phenomenological" has been used increasingly in the social sciences to refer to perspectives that are concerned with the subject's point of view, with meaning, subjectivity, or consciousness—perspectives that account for "the phenomenon" under investigation as irreducible and autonomous in its own right.

In phenomenological or other interpretive studies, the researcher pays close attention to the lived experience of the research subject's world, facilitating development of the subject's story and the older person's definitions of meaning. Research becomes a collaborative endeavor which Frank (1980) has called "the collaborative creation of meaning." The researcher allows and guides the subject to develop ideas, models, and cognitive schemes in order to generate and elucidate meaningful categories of knowledge, being, and inquiry. The subject's story, or narrative, becomes the most important research finding. Its structure, content, purpose, and style are the focus of investigation and interpretation.

Recent works in gerontology employing these approaches include

Abel (1990), Kaufman (1988c), Mannheimer (1991), Mullen (1992), and Rubinstein (1989, 1990). Phenomenological and other interpretive approaches to gerontological research allow us to learn the language, the categories of meaning of older persons themselves. Those approaches enable the voices of the elderly to be heard in ways they have not been, so that we, as researchers and practitioners, are able to see dimensions of aging—like the ageless self—that were previously invisible to us.

Note

1. National Institute on Aging research grant no. AG04053. Gay Becker, P.I., 1983–1986; Sharon Kaufman, P.I., 1988–1991.

References

Abel, E., 1990. *Daughters Caring for Elderly Parents*. In J. F. Gubrium and A. Sankar, eds., *The Home Care Experience: Ethnography and Policy*. Newbury Park, CA: Sage.

Becker, G., 1993. "Continuity After a Stroke: Implications of Life-Course Disruption in Old Age." *Gerontologist* 33: 148–58.

Becker, G. and Kaufman, S., 1986. *Socio-Cultural Mechanisms of Rehabilitation in Old Age: Final Report*. Grant #AG04053, Washington, D.C.: National Institute on Aging.

Frank, G., 1980. "Life Histories in Gerontology: The Subjective Side to Aging." In C. Fry and J. Keith, eds., *New Methods for Old Age Research*. Chicago: Loyola University Press.

Frank, G., 1986. "On Embodiment: A Case Study of Congenital Limb Deficiency in American Culture." *Culture, Medicine, and Psychiatry* 10:189–219.

Kastenbaum, R., 1987. "Gerontology's Search for Understanding." *Gerontologist* 18:59–63.

Kaufman, S. R., 1986. *The Ageless Self: Sources of Meaning in Late Life*. Madison: University of Wisconsin Press.

Kaufman, S. R., 1988a. "Stroke Rehabilitation and the Negotiation of Identity." In S. Reinharz and G. Rowles, eds., *Qualitative Gerontology*. New

York: Springer Publishing Co.

Kaufman, S. R., 1988b. "Illness, Biography, and the Interpretation of Self Following a Stroke." *Journal of Aging Studies* 2:217–27.

Kaufman, S. R., 1988c. "Toward a Phenomenology of Boundaries in Medicine: Chronic Illness Experience in the Case of Stroke." *Medical Anthropology Quarterly* 2(4): 338–54.

Mannheimer, R. J., 1991. "In Search of the Gerontological Self." Paper presented at the 44th Annual Scientific Meeting of the Gerontological Society of America, San Francisco.

Moody, H. R., 1988. "Toward a Critical Gerontology: The Contribution of the Humanities to Theories of Aging." In J. E. Birren and V. L. Bengtson, eds., *Emergent Theories of Aging*. New York: Springer.

Mullen, P. B., 1992. Listening to Old Voices: *Folklore, Life Stories, and the Elderly*. Urbana: University of Illinois Press.

Neugarten, B. L., 1977. "Personality and Aging." In J. E. Birren and K. W. Schaie, eds., *Handbook of the Psychology of Aging*. New York: Van Nostrand Reinhold.

Neugarten, B. L., 1984. "Interpretive Social Science and Research on Aging." In A. Rossi, ed., *Gender and the Life Course*. Chicago: Aldine.

Rubinstein, R. L., 1989. "Themes in the Meaning of Care Giving." *Journal of Aging Studies* 3(2): 119–38.

Rubinstein, R. L., 1990. "Personal Identity and Environmental Meaning in Later Life." *Journal of Aging Studies* 4(2): 131–47.

Tornstam, L., 1992. "The Quo Vadis of Gerontology: On the Scientific Paradigm of Gerontology." *Gerontologist* 32(3): 318–26.

Erik Erikson

Ages, Stages, and Stories

Steven Weiland

rik H. Erikson became a psychoanalyst and life cycle theorist by chance. He had a brief career as an artist. In his mid-20s he became a teacher of art, history, and other subjects to young children in an unusual school, the one associated with the Vienna Psychoanalytic Institute where the new vocation of child psychoanalysis emerged under the leadership of Freud's daughter Anna. Erikson earned a certificate in Montessori education just before enrolling in the Institute. When he emigrated to America in the mid-1930s, Erikson had a difficult time in establishing a psychoanalytic career. Unlike his American colleagues, he was without an academic degree or an M.D., and he was still a newcomer to English. But today no developmental theory is better known than Erikson's. The eight-stage chart of the life cycle that appeared in the first edition of *Childhood and Society* (1950) is a familiar image in virtually every textbook of human development, taking its place in a long history of life cycle iconography (Cole, 1992). Even influential developmental theorists who disagree with Erikson's approach call it "probably the single most important theory of adult personality development....Erikson's views of adulthood...have become received wisdom in all their details" (McCrae and Costa, 1990, pp. 11–12).

For many years Erikson's theory was best known for its designation of the "identity crisis" of adolescence. But as Erikson himself has aged, he has given greater priority to adulthood and late life. He has supplied to our imagery of aging his own intellectual and cultural presence—especially in the interviews and photographs of his late years—as an exemplary elder reflecting his own theoretical ideals of generativity and integrity (Brenman-Gibson, 1984; Erikson and Erikson, 1981; Goleman, 1988; Hall, 1983).

The purpose of this chapter is first to propose that a durable imagery of aging can be found in stage-structured developmental theory itself and then to show how Erikson has sought to see beyond the original intentions of his most familiar formulation. Even as he continued to work within the format of a stage-structured psychology, he found opportunities to extend its meanings and to propose that complementary forms of developmental inquiry and imagery—especially in narrative (or biography) and film—were essential to his theory.

IMAGES OF HUMAN FULFILLMENT

Erikson's theory is stage-structured but not explicitly age-linked; the relations between the stages can only be approximated. They are organized into a system of polarities that tempt us to think about psychological dynamics in a form that is more binary than Erikson intended. For example, following the core conflict of the sixth stage or the period of early adulthood (about age 25–45) that yields "intimacy" as its strength, the core developmental dialectic for middle adulthood or the seventh stage (about age 45–65) is "Generativity vs. Stagnation." "Care" is the strength that emerges from this internal conflict, *within* the characteristic dynamic of the stage and *between* that stage and the others in the life cycle. Generativity is, simply enough, the capacity to provide for succeeding generations. Indeed, the life cycle itself is what Erikson calls "a system of generation and regeneration" that is given continuity by domestic, professional, and other institutions. The eighth stage completes the cycle with a new conflict and a reassertion of developmental themes from all previous stages. "Integrity" is the antithesis of "Despair," and the strength that emerges from their interaction is "Wisdom."

In this normative scheme, "Wisdom" is a function of the gradual maturation of "Integrity," a capacious frame of mind. It is "the tendency to keep things together," to strengthen the self, its relations with others and the past. The integrative way of late life means "comradeship with the ordering ways of distant times and different pursuits, as expressed in their simple products and sayings" (Erikson, 1982, p. 65). By this Erikson means especially religious tradition (e.g., 1981), a feature of Erikson's work that has not been emphasized in the secular world of academic research in human development (for some exceptions, see Seeber, 1990).

The stage-structured approach can appear rigid and deterministic, normative in its hierarchy of stage-specific traits, and totalizing in its intentions. Erikson's seeming willingness to concede developmental ideals to any society's "dominant conception of the phases of life" has prompted some critics to judge him too compliant within the framework of prevailing social values (e.g., Gutmann, 1974; Roazen, 1980). The dialectical model of development has been criticized as insufficiently contextualized, even as "context" itself ("society" in its many manifestations for Erikson) has been identified as a term needing greater rigor in its developmental applications (Dannefer, 1992). There is an unmistakably teleological cast to Erikson's ideas, which, while providing for considerable variability in development, may not recognize enough "plasticity" in the individual's complex interactions with the environment (Lerner, 1984). Within the study of human development, Erikson's work must be understood as problematic in the several senses identified by the debate over psychological and sociological models of the life span (Dannefer, 1984; Featherman and Lerner, 1985). That is, even a relativist developmental theory, in which historical change is asserted to be a key variable, still needs to guard against the "reduction" of behavior to psychology.

Developmental psychologists interested in adulthood and aging have generally been kinder to Erikson than have the sociologists (e.g., Ryff and Migdal, 1984). Still, the verifiability of Erikson's theory is only one way of accounting for the interest that scientists and scholars may have in it. In a candid essay, Carol Ryff offered a historical account of her research and the role of stage-structured theory. She notes first that "those who continued to endorse stage models were deemed naive and had to suffer the embarrassment of advocating theories that were uncommonly neat and tidy." She rejects the idea that it was the orderliness of the theory that mattered most, and she explains the durability of her commitment to the stage-structured view by identifying a motive nominally remote from the routines of academic behavioral science.

The attraction was that [stage-structured theories] formulated spiraling progressions of improvement for the individual. Each theorist had formulated ways in which the individual could continue to develop, to become more differentiated, and function at a higher level. It was this quality, these spiraling progressions of improvement, that captured and sustained my interest. Admittedly, such conceptions of personal improvement are likely to be sprinkled with individual differences, cohort effects, and cultural variability, but such effects do not discount the impact these models have as guiding ideals that influence what people become and how they develop. Such images of human fulfillment are central to understanding how we conceive life-span development. (Ryff, 1985, p. 99)

Because her data do not demand either complete vindication or refutation of the stage-structured view, Ryff calls for developmental theory that stands between the false ideal of complete orderliness and the view that there is no underlying developmental structure of personality and cognitive development in adulthood.

The quest for a gerontological theory of the "middle range," as Bernice Neugarten (1985) recommended, is reflected too in the work of other leading developmentalists. Paul Baltes (1987) is careful to recognize Erikson's influence, though he expresses some ambivalence about the totalizing nature of his theory. Instead he names a "family" of methods that make up the "life-span perspective" and he has signified a central goal of such a reconceptualization by turning to the study of "wisdom," another image of human fulfillment even if tentatively detached from the apparent teleology of the Eriksonian model. The point, as personality psychologist Ryff asserts, is that in order to address the most profound meanings of human experience, a life-span view is indispensable, and however formulated (for example, by a cognitive and experimental psychologist like Baltes), it will carry overtones from Erikson's work.

So too are "images of human fulfillment" at the core of Thomas Cole's recent historical account of *The Journey of Life* (1992). This study is especially timely in illustrating paradoxes and possibilities in Erikson's role in gerontological inquiry and practice. For Cole the influence of stage- and age-structured views has often tended to reduce the historical role of religion and spirituality in explaining and guiding the life course. By urging a renewal of such values, Cole implicitly directs us to the elements of Erikson's theory that make such possibilities part of developmental theory. Erikson has made religion and spiritual life a central subject in his influential psychohistorical studies of Luther and Gandhi in order to show how human values are made and remade as part of a life history that is understandable if not pre-

22

dictable according to principles of human development. These studies add concreteness to his stage theory as they prompt us to subordinate the (misleading) attractions of a calibrated maturity to an appreciation of historical and social contingency.

When he titled his best-known book *Childhood and Society*, Erikson meant most obviously to propose that the former is defined by the latter, that society is a "context" (however problematic [Dannefer, 1992]) that must be accounted for in understanding human development. But the first term can also be said to help define the second, as developmental ideas and ideals help to shape human communities. Erikson has always insisted on "historical relativism" in thinking about problems of inquiry and method. Accordingly, his theory is itself an invitation to address how it needs to be revised to meet the circumstances of new generations.

FROM CHART TO STORY

To be sure, Erikson has relied on the eight-stage representation of the life cycle throughout his career, noting in the mid-1980s that he had learned over the years the value of the chart in "keeping a theory together." It amounted to recognition of "how difficult it is even for highly trained individuals to keep in mind the logic of a contextual conceptualization of developmental matters" (1984, p. 157). The chart and the discursive symmetry of the formulation of the eight stages of development—with its dialectical pairs of terms—inevitably came to represent his theory as a highly schematized one. No doubt that accounts for part of its appeal, in addition to what it may have done to inspire developmental psychologists themselves. Precisely because it offers a seemingly bounded and coherent image of human growth and change, it is well suited to textbook accounts of development and to the purposes of practitioners in many fields unfamiliar with the complexities—clinical, historical, rhetorical—that Erikson himself became aware of as his work gained a large audience across the academic disciplines in the 1960s and 1970s. Accordingly, he himself has sought to see beyond his initial formulation while preserving its essential features.

Erikson's theorizing has always displayed a large range of methods and subjects. In Childhood and Society he used the clinical interview; observational techniques (of play therapy); projective tests; anthropological fieldwork; literary, historical, and biographical analysis; and even a detailed account of a film (about the Soviet writer Maxim

23

Gorky). Erikson joined the anthropologist Margaret Mead and the sociologist David Riesman, his colleagues and friends, in addressing scholarly and scientific themes using film.

When Erikson joined the Harvard faculty in 1960, he initiated what became a famous course in the human life cycle reflecting the eclectic methods of *Childhood and Society*. For "data" he turned to Ingmar Bergman's film *Wild Strawberries* (1958), which became the subject of two long essays he published late in his career, each being an occasion for restatement of his theory though now in the unique setting that a narrative example could provide. He says in the first that though "a good story does not need a chart to come alive...a chart...especially one with so many empty boxes, can use a good story" (1978, p. 30). And as I have noted, Erikson's biographies indicate that during the 1950s and 1960s—when his stage-structured theory was gaining advocates—he had been moving "from chart to story" as his career presented opportunities to add examples and meaning to his theory. When Erikson turned in the 1970s and 1980s to the study of late life, he used narrative to bring its themes to clinical, academic, and public attention.

In *Wild Strawberries* a 78-year-old Swedish professor and biomedical researcher (also a physician) makes a day-long automobile trip to Lund to be honored by the university there for 50 years of achievement. The journey is rich in memories, dreams, and symbolic material recounted by Dr. Borg as a series of entries in his journal following his return to Stockholm. In his studies of the film Erikson (1978; Erikson, Erikson and Kivnick, 1986) follows the day's remembered events closely and uses the eight stages didactically, believing as he does in the representative meaning of Bergman's story. In the dream that opens the film Borg appears to anticipate his own death. On the journey itself he encounters painful memories of his family, his first romantic love and disappointment, his training as a physician and doubts about his professional identity, and the agony associated with his marriage, his wife having rejected him for his coldness. The journey, with its nominally joyous rationale, is presented (one might say dialectically) with a strong sense of estrangement and regret. These are reflected too in Dr. Borg's poor relations with his son and daughter-in-law who, significantly enough given the attention in the film to the problem of generativity (versus stagnation), are struggling over the decision to have a child.

It is easy to see why Dr. Borg impressed Erikson as a virtual case study of those who move through the last stage of life "mourning not only for time forfeited and space depleted but also for autonomy weakened, initiative lost, intimacy missed, generativity neglected—not to speak of identity potentials bypassed, or indeed, an all-too-limiting identity lived" (Erikson and Erikson, 1982, p. 63). While he has been a success in his professional life, Borg has failed in personal and family relations. Precisely because he is overdefined intellectually, Borg needs to recover his capacity for feeling, which the film's encounters—in their actuality and psychological derivations—prompt him to do. As the film ends Borg is reconciled with his son and daughter-in-law. And in the final frames he dreams again, this time of his parents in a pastoral image of early childhood filial happiness.

The life cycle is reversed in the film's telling in the sense that the experiences of childhood, youth, and early adulthood are not seen as conclusively formative but as parts of a personality "configuration" that can be reshaped near the end of life. For Erikson, Bergman solved a formal problem that had come to preoccupy the psychoanalyst in his later years, namely, the proper sequence in which to present the eight stages. In his last two books (Erikson and Erikson, 1982; Erikson, Erikson and Kivnick, 1986) Erikson reverses the order of presentation in order to give priority to adult development and aging, to signify that generative potentials are available to make individual life a true cycle with overlapping strengths binding infancy and old age and the generations too. And in keeping with the increasing importance of religion and spirituality as themes in his work, Erikson asserts that the youngest and the oldest are bound together by their relation to the "numinous" or the "ultimate other." For the infant or small child the mother supplies the "aura of a hallowed presence." For the aged in the last stage of life, such experience brings assurance of "separateness transcended and yet also of distinctiveness confirmed, and thus of the very basis of the sense of 'I'" (Erikson and Erikson, 1982, p. 45). "Faith" serves the old like "hope" the young. Thus is Dr. Borg's life cycle completed. Erikson comments on the meaning of the last part of the film in terms of his theoretical position: "As we thus recognize the contraries which arise in every individual as the necessary correlates of human strength, we may well pause to consider the special function which the more inclusive visions of the great religions and ideologies have had in daily life, namely to counteract the divisive potential arising in every stage of human growth" (1978, p. 17).

Wild Strawberries is a redemptive narrative and Dr. Borg's life history (or "life review" as it is now often called) is well fitted to Erikson's stages. But it strains the chart too with the ambiguous resources of narrative, spiritual meanings, and cinematic imagery. The last especially—in the wisdom, solace, and rest observable in the visage of honored, troubled, but then reconciled Dr. Borg—helps to convince us of the uses of the theory. As a life story *Wild Strawberries* has form and direction as the theory requires, but so too does it reveal how overdefined symmetries in the chart (as Erikson recognized) direct us to the complex unity and contingencies of lived experience. Erikson and other recent psychological interpreters of the film (Cohen-Shalov, 1992; Cohler, 1992; Rosel, 1988) stress Dr. Borg's mental achievements, the meaning he finds in his past as a function of gaining greater control over the present and future. He seems to be summing things up in accord with the demands of the stage-structured theory of late life. But as Erikson asserts in a theoretical vein near the end of his first analysis of *Wild Strawberries,* "Any fulfillment of the individual life cycle, far from being simply a matter of finding terminal clarity, can only fulfill what is given in the order of things by remaining responsible and by contributing continuous solutions to the ongoing cycle of generations" (1978, p. 29).

The film helps us to focus too on the human reconciliations that bring Borg belated satisfaction. A chart cannot dramatize such moments nor can it demonstrate their universality. Those are the virtues of art and narrative and the images of aging they provide. Gerontological and scholarly and (even) scientific interest in narratives now show signs of unity based on investigating how such "acts of meaning," in Jerome Bruner's suggestive phrase, are foundational to cognition and identity (Bruner, 1990; Cohler, 1992; Manheimer, 1989). In Erikson's view these "acts" derive in part from the impulse to create "model situations," forms even of play, which help us to master reality. But he knows too that stories, life reviews, films, and other genres have a purposeful epistemology. In our narratives we "inventively anticipate the future from the vantage point of a corrected and shared past as we redeem our failures and strengthen our hopes" (1982, p. 51).

Erikson acknowledges that Dr. Borg's life history can be unified around the "inner logic" of psychological theory, but its meaning and utility depend too on other sources of coherence. It is "held together...by a pervasive realism, a tender earthiness in all its characters and a sometimes ironical appreciation of their existence at their age in that spot on earth in that period of cultural and historical determination. It is this that makes them prototypical for human beings in other times and places and thus existential in the most concrete sense of the word" (1978, p. 3). With his essays on *Wild Strawberries*, Erikson fulfilled the distinctive contribution to psychoanalysis predicted by Anna Freud. For when Erikson expressed to her his doubts about the fate of his original artistic vocation and his qualifications for a new career, she replied that psychoanalysis would need those who could make skeptics "see."

CONCLUSION: PROBLEMS OF BEING

Moving beyond the most familiar features of Erikson's stage-structured theory is no more difficult than recognizing Erikson's own efforts to make it more complex and supple. As he himself aged, he adapted and extended his theory (Weiland, 1989). By the time of *The Life Cycle Completed* (1982) he had made a career based on reconciling diverse strains of psychoanalysis, developmental psychology, biography, religious inquiry, and cultural criticism. These are now all resources for understanding Erikson's distinctive contribution.

When he looked back at the origins of his vocation, Erikson reasserted its clinical format and "healing authority." But with his life cycle theory and its application to stories, Erikson himself has been instrumental in making developmental and narrative perspectives central to late twentieth-century uses of psychoanalysis. He is, perhaps paradoxically for our culture's preoccupation with age and cultural difference, dedicated to historical relativism and to what binds the generations. Understood dialectically, however, these ideals present differences with their own generative potential.

Bergman himself believed that the painful experiences of childhood and other stages are "so blocked they're immobile, impossible to handle" (1973, pp. 147–48). His film, as Erikson demonstrates, belies this view and offers images of aging and reconciliation based on the reintegration of incomplete identity struggles. As a narrative, it subordinates theory to experience. Erikson's treatment of *Wild Strawberries* shows how theoretical constructs can guide developmental interpretations that include skepticism about their meaning and application. For Erikson has always been determined to reach beyond the apparent lim-

27

its of his innovation toward what may not be expressible in theoretical discourse or for that matter in language of any kind (Weiland, 1992). The most compelling ideas about aging are those deriving from encounters with it that defy discursive representation and invite us to "see" deeply into human experience: "We must recognize an Existential Identity which our identity theories cannot fathom: these are all problems of Being, the open or disguised presence of which we must learn to discern in the everyday involvements of old people" (1984, p. 163).

References

Baltes, P., 1987. "Theoretical Propositions of Life-Span Developmental Psychology: On the Dynamics Between Growth and Decline." *Developmental Psychology* 23: 611–26.

Bergman, I., 1973. *Bergman on Bergman: Interviews with Ingmar Bergman.* Translated from the Swedish by Paul B. Austin. London: Secker and Warburg.

Brenman-Gibson, M., 1984. "Erik Erikson and the Ethics of Survival." *Harvard Magazine*, November-December, pp. 59–64.

Bruner, J., 1990. *Acts of Meaning.* Cambridge: Harvard University Press.

Cohen-Shalev, A., 1992. "The Effect of Aging on Dramatic Realization of Old Age: The Example of Ingmar Bergman." *Gerontologist* 32: 739–43.

Cohler, B., 1992. "Aging, Morale, and Meaning: The Nexus of Narrative." In T. Cole, W. A. Achenbaum, P. Jacobi and R. Kastenbaum, eds., *Voices and Visions of Aging: Toward a Critical Gerontology.* New York: Springer Publishing Co..

Cole, T., 1992. *The Journey of Life: A Cultural History of Aging in America.* Cambridge, Mass.: Cambridge University Press.

Dannefer, D., 1984. "Adult Development and Social Theory: A Paradigmatic Reappraisal." *American Sociological Review* 49: 100–116.

Dannefer, D., 1992. "On the Conceptualization of Context in Developmental Discourse: Four Meanings of Context and Their Implications." In D. L. Featherman, R. M. Lerner and M. Perlmutter, eds., *Life-Span Development and Behavior* 11: 83–111.

Erikson, E. H., 1950, 1963. *Childhood and Society.* New York: Norton.

Erikson, E. H., 1968. Identity: *Youth and Crisis.* New York: Norton.

Erikson, E. H., 1978. "Reflections on Dr. Borg's Life Cycle." In E. H. Erikson, ed., *Adulthood.* New York: Norton

Erikson, E. H., 1981. "The Galilean Sayings and the Sense of 'I.'" *Yale Review* 70: 321–62.

Erikson, E. H., 1982. *The Life Cycle Completed: A Review.* New York: Norton

Erikson, E. H., 1984. "Reflections on the Last Stage—and the First." *Psychoanalytic Study of the Child* 39(1): 55–65.

Erikson, E. H., and Erikson, J., 1981. "On Generativity and Identity: From a Conversation with Erik and Joan Erikson." *Harvard Educational Review* 51: 249–69.

Erikson, E. H., Erikson, J. and Kivnick, H., 1986. *Vital Involvement in Old Age.* New York: Norton.

Featherman, D., and Lerner, R., 1985. "Ontogenesis and Sociogenesis: Problematics for Theory and Research about Development and Socialization." *American Sociological Review* 50: 659–76.

Goleman, D., 1988. "Erikson, in His Own Old Age, Expands His View of Life." *New York Times,* 14 June, II, 13,16.

Gutmann, D., 1974. "Erik Erikson's America." *Commentary* 58 (September): 60–64.

Hall, E., 1983. "A Conversation with Erik Erikson." *Psychology Today* 17(6): 32–39.

Lemer, R., 1984. *On the Nature of Human Plasticity.* New York: Cambridge University Press.

Manheimer, R., 1989. "The Narrative Quest in Qualitative Gerontology." *Journal of Aging Studies* 3: 231–52.

McCrae, R., and Costa, P., Jr., 1990. *Personality in Adulthood.* New York: Guilford.

Neugarten, B., 1985. "Interpretive Social Science and Research on Aging." In A. Rossi, ed., *Gender and the Life Course.* New York: Aldine.

Roazen, P., 1980. "Erik H. Erikson's America: The Political Implications of Ego Psychology." *Journal of the History of the Behavioral Sciences* 16: 333–41.

Rosel, N., 1988. "Clarification and Application of Erik Erikson's Eighth Stage of Man." *International Journal of Aging and Human Development* 27: 11–23.

Ryff, C., 1985. "The Subjective Experience of Life-Span Transitions." In A. Rossi, ed., *Gender and the Life Course.* New York: Aldine.

Ryff, C., and Migdal, S., 1984. "Intimacy and Generativity: Self-Perceived Transitions." *Signs: The Journal of Women and Culture* 9: 470–81.

Seeber, J., ed., 1990. *Spiritual Maturity in the Later Years.* New York: Haworth.

Weiland, S., 1989. "Aged Erikson: The Completion of the Life Cycle." *Journal of Aging Studies* 3: 253–62.

Weiland, S., 1992. "Psychoanalysis Without Words: Erik H. Erikson's American Apprenticeship." *Michigan Quarterly Review* 31: 1–18.

CHAPTER FOUR

Simone de Beauvoir

Prospects for the Future of Older Women

Kathleen Woodward

Simone de Beauvoir—political activist, lifelong partner of French philosopher Jean-Paul Sartre, and author of many novels and memoirs—is arguably the most influential feminist of the twentieth-century West. She is celebrated primarily, of course, for *The Second Sex*, a passionate treatise on women that appeared in 1949 and remains today required reading in college courses in women's studies across the United States.

That Beauvoir also is the author of what I think could have been an equally influential book on aging is virtually unknown, however. Researched and written when she was on the edge of 60, this monumental (if somewhat rambling) book explores the roots of what we today call ageism from social, economic, and psychological perspectives. Published under the unambiguous title *La Vieillesse (Old Age)* in France, where it quickly became a best seller, the book appeared in 1972 in the United States under the misleading title *The Coming of Age*—as if to coax unwilling readers to the dismaying subject of old age by promising them a birthday cake with 21 candles on it.

In general *The Coming of Age* was attacked by reviewers (most of them men, as far as I can determine) for its unrelievedly pessimistic view of aging. The eminent psychologist Robert Coles (1972) complained that Beauvoir "never wants her reader to look forward to old age," condemning her as "a strong, unsparing, at times outraged and bitterly scornful writer." Even sharper in his criticism, the distinguished gerontologist Robert N. Butler (1972) charged that Beauvoir "literally detests aging and the older person in herself." At the same time the book was ignored by feminists in the United States largely, I think, because at that moment in history the women's movement was concerned with reproductive rights, childcare, and equal job opportunities—issues linked with the earlier years of female adulthood. Censured by some, neglected by others, *The Coming of Age* went out of print.

With the distance of some 20 years, I want to briefly reconsider Beauvoir's negative portrayal of aging—particularly of aging as a woman—in the light of some of her other writing and in terms of her own life as an older woman: She was active as a writer and public figure until she died in 1986 at the age of 78. For if *The Coming of Age* is an acute critical analysis of ageism, it is also a symptom of the very anxieties a particular woman—Simone de Beauvoir—associated with aging; it is an eloquent expression of the fears of aging to which women especially are subject. If Beauvoir trenchantly theorized that the older person in Western culture is constructed as the devalued Other, as a grim stranger to our "real" selves, she also unconsciously internalized that very figure of the older woman as dreadful. In a sense Butler was right: Beauvoir did detest the older woman in herself. I am convinced that one of the reasons for this sorry failure is that Beauvoir did not have at hand what she would have regarded as positive models of older women by which to plot the prospects of her own future.

Although *The Coming of Age* does not focus on aging from the point of view of gender, Beauvoir does flatly assert: "I have never come across one single woman, either in life or in books who has looked upon her old age cheerfully" (p. 297). Although she refers in *The Coming of Age* to the experience of aging of many celebrated older men (artists, writers, political leaders), she does not mention many older women (Madame de Sévigné, Lou Andreas-Salomé, and Colette are among the few). Her reading of cultural history, in other words, did not yield a pivotal and varied range of possibilities of what life as an older prominent woman could be. At the age of 62, Beauvoir surveyed the generation older than herself and concluded morosely that loneliness and unhappiness were to be her legacy from it. Even the generation of leaders below her own generation gave her no comfort, perhaps because she saw it as constituted of complacent old men, not women. Although lengthy, this telling passage from *The Coming of Age* deserves to be quoted here:

> Even at my age, my relationship with the various generations has quite changed: there is one left older than mine; it is exceedingly sparse, and death lies in wait for it. My own, once so busily teeming, has been severely thinned. What I used to look upon as the young generation is now made up of mature men, fathers and even grandfathers, thoroughly settled in life. If I want to know the really youthful point of view on some subject, I have to ask the generation below. In a few years I shall reach what Madame de Sévigné called "the position of the oldest member in our family." From that stage onwards there is the threat of loneliness and the unhappiness that comes with it." (p. 435)

That Simone de Beauvoir identified primarily with men and that she associated aging with powerlessness (both in terms of physical strength and in terms of political, cultural, and economic influence) is also clearly seen in the parable of Buddha with which she opens her book. At a critical moment in his youth, he encountered what was to him a disconcerting figure, "a tottering, wrinkled, toothless, white-haired man, bowed, mumbling and trembling as he propped himself along on his stick" (p. 1). Upon being informed that this was "what it meant to be old," Buddha stoically determined to take on "the entirety of the human state" (p. 1). My point is this: When Beauvoir counsels us as readers of *The Coming of Age* to *identify* with an older man or an older woman, it is this image of *old* that she has definitely in her mind's eye—a person powerless and frail, inarticulate and dispossessed. A strong older person—a person with a rich emotional, intellectual, and sexual life, a person physically vital and mentally energetic, a person linked by such strengths to other generations—this was unimaginable to her.

In an interview given when she was 69, Beauvoir affirmed the particular importance for women of autobiography, in her view closer to the bone of reality than fiction. Beauvoir firmly believed that "only a woman can write what it is to feel as a woman, to be a woman" (Jardine, 1979). Autobiography can reveal how women feel "from within"—their subjectivity, their sensibility. So I want to turn back to the closing pages of her memoir *The Prime of Life* (1963), published when she was 55, because these final words, which so shocked her readers with their tone of depressive fatality, express her feelings then about aging as a woman.

The "most irreparable thing" that has happened to her since 1944 when Paris was liberated from the Germans, she confesses levelly if dully, is that she has grown old. I must acknowledge that some of her feelings associated with aging are politicized and, to my mind, mature. She understands that in growing older she has shed the optimistic and idealistic conviction of youth that suffering in the world can be eradicated through political activism. In a sense, then, the deaths around the world from political conflict and callousness weigh on her more now. Such human misery, "made absolute," overwhelms her (p. 654). She feels it keenly, but perhaps too piercingly for it to be only wise insight into the human condition. For in more obviously personal terms, aging for Beauvoir is a form of *shrinking, petrifaction*, and *rotting*—these are the metaphors she uses. She despairs that she will ever make love with a man again. As I visualize her writing these pages, I see her becoming virtually hysterical as she imagines her bleak future—no new desires, imminent deterioration.

How can we explain the force of her fear? Her six-year-long love affair with Claude Lanzmann, a man much younger than she, had come to an end not too many years before her book was published. Although she does not mention him here by name, she does write, "the moment has come to say: Never again! It is not I who am saying good-bye to all those things I once enjoyed, it is they who are leaving me" (p. 657). Perhaps she was still suffering from this loss—or others. But more significant to me in comprehending the underpinning of her violent fears of aging is the way she understands her relationships to other generations. As for a generation older than her own, she does not even imagine one here. In these last six pages of *The Prime of Life* she does not write about anyone older than she is—and remember, she was only 55 when this book appeared. For her, there is only young and old. The people who are her contemporaries are old, shockingly so. She writes, appalled: "That hoary-headed gentleman, who looks like one of my great- uncles, tells me with a smile that we used to play together in the gardens of the Luxembourg" (p. 655). For her, old is monolithic, that is, it has only to do with withering away, and her 50-some-year-old body has already been "attacked by the pox of time for which there is no cure" (p. 656). Here we have again, then, another instance of Beauvoir not being able to draw on any powerful models of older women who have preceded her. For her, there is no genealogy of older women to support her sense of an open future.

As for the generation younger than her own, she imagines that they see her as irrelevant; worse, as already dead: "In the eyes of those twenty-year-olds, I see myself already dead and mummified" (p. 654) She has internalized what she takes to be the gaze of youth and, now middle-aged, she turns its violence against herself. Why else would she be so vulnerable to this comment by a young woman: "'you remind me of my mother,' I am told by a woman of about thirty or so" (p. 655). Why should this necessarily be so threatening, so frightening, a nightmare in the midst of waking life? Beauvoir tells us this dream, which fulfills her wish for youth (it is waking "reality" that is her nightmare): "Often in my sleep I dream that in a dream I'm fifty-four, I wake and find I'm only thirty. 'What a terrible nightmare I had!' says the young woman who thinks she's awake" (p. 656). And what is that "reality" in Beauvoir's eyes? She hates her own image—"the eyebrows slipping down toward the eyes, the bags underneath, the excessive fullness of the cheeks, that air of sadness around the mouth that wrinkles always bring" (p. 656). Thus, feeling no connection with those older than herself, feeling estranged from those of her own generation, feeling threatened by those younger than herself, Beauvoir is cut off from the reciprocal vector of generational continuity, stranded. Suffocating, she feels crushed by time itself.

At 40, Beauvoir was terrified by the prospect of 50. At 50, she feared being 60. As I read her novella *The Age of Discretion*, published in France in 1967 when she was 59, I find again a woman who does not feel compelling connections to generations older and younger. The main character is a 60-year-old woman very much like Beauvoir herself—a writer, a political activist of fierce and uncompromising convictions, a woman of volatile emotions. Like Beauvoir, this woman is flooded with fears of aging. She thinks of her husband, who is the same age as herself, as older than she is. When she goes to the market, she finds herself gazing obsessively at women older than herself: "The little old lady hobbled from one stall to another, her sparse hair carefully combed back, her hand grasping the handle of her empty basket. In earlier days I never used to worry about old people: I looked upon them as the dead whose legs still kept moving. Now I see them—men and women: only a little older than myself." The future she imagines for herself in the shape of this "little old lady" is one of ill health and poverty, both financial and emotional.

Interestingly enough, however, unlike, Beauvoir, the main character in *The Age of Discretion* has a child (Beauvoir never had any children) and a mother-in-law. It is as if in this literary space Beauvoir provides herself with a three-generational family in order to imagine what a difference that might make. Furthermore, in this novella, which is narrated in the first person as if it were autobiography, Beauvoir also provides her heroine with a close friend who is much younger than herself, a woman who is one of her former students and is (the main character realizes with a start) now 40 years old. How does this 60-year-old woman—Beauvoir gives her no name—come to understand her relation to her own generation as well as her relation to the generations beyond and below hers? As I have already suggested, she feels alienated from her husband, André; by the end of the story, they do reconcile—in good part because he has regained some of his enthusiasm for life, that is to say, he has grown "younger" in her eyes. What of friends her own age? She does not seem to have any and furthermore tells us that she likes younger women better because "their curiosity spurs mine into life: they draw me into their future, on the far side of my own grave" (p. 21), as if to say that women her own age were on the brink of imminent death.

What of the younger generation? She breaks violently with her son who has decided to pursue a career she does not approve of, feeling contempt for the future he is shaping for himself. She gives her latest book, which she has worked on hard for three years and is convinced is her best by far, to her younger friend Martine, and is cut to the quick when Martine appraises it judiciously as a restatement of past ideas rather than as a wholly new and original piece of work. In the course of the story, she does not see Martine again.

Most significant, however, is the way in which this 60-year-old woman does not absorb the example of a vigorous older woman represented by her 84-year-old mother-in-law. Active in local politics, healthy, intellectually engaged, this older woman lives alone. She reads a great deal, she gardens, she speaks her mind combatively. When André tells his wife that this indeed is the best part of his mother's life, his wife is dryly cynical and sarcastic, responding: "'Certainly. It's one of those hard cases in which old age is a happy period—old age after a hard life, one that has more or less been eaten up by others'" (p. 72). On balance this 84-year-old woman is represented as vital, as in fact disappointed in the younger generation for its lack of involvement in social issues! But how does her daughter-in-law imagine her subjectivity? "Age had not taken her powers away; but deep inside her, what went on? Did she think of death? With resignation? With dread? I dared not ask" (p.

74). That she does not inquire how this woman in fact does feel is telling. She projects her own fears of aging onto her, in effect dismissing the experience of this older woman as irrelevant to her own future.

The novella closes with the by now familiar dark prospect of aging as a woman, a prospect that Beauvoir, it seems, could not shake. "Would the dread of aging," she intones, "take hold of me again? Do not look too far ahead. Ahead there were the horrors of death and farewells: it was false teeth, sciatica, infirmity, intellectual bareness, loneliness in a strange world that we would no longer understand and that would carry on without us. Shall I succeed in not lifting my gaze to these horizons? Or shall I learn to behold them without horror?" (p. 85). These grim rhetorical questions are never answered. It is as if Beauvoir, as an author, sent herself a message in *The Age of Discretion* that she herself could not absorb. Her 60-year-old character feels no affinity with this impressive woman a generation older. She does not "see" the positive model that Beauvoir had imagined for her. And who is "her"? It seems to be Beauvoir herself.

The thrilling irony is that Beauvoir's last years—up to her death at 78—were marked by intellectual vigor and a striking lack of attenuated physical debility. Her own experience put the lie to her lifelong fears of old age. In 1973 at the age of 65, she started a section on feminism in the periodical *Les Temps Modernes*. During these years she granted many interviews, and a film on her life was made. In 1981 she published an unflinching account of Sartre's long illness and death, which appeared in the United States under the title *Adieux: A Farewell to Sartre*. She also edited a collection of letters by Sartre to her and others, published in 1983. She formed close friendships with women younger than herself.

In a sense, then, Beauvoir herself followed the advice she gave in *The Coming of Age*: "to go on pursuing ends that give our existence a meaning—devotion to individuals, to groups or to causes, social, political, intellectual, or creative work" (p. 540). Her own later years proved an example of her maxim that one's life has value so long as one attributes value to the life of others, by means of love, friendship, indignation, compassion" (p. 541). And so if in her long life she could never imagine for herself a sustaining genealogy of powerful older women, she has bequeathed that to us. Many of us, in fact, may only remember her as an older woman. The French intellectual Catherine Clément (1979), for example, writing words of praise of the 71-year-old Beauvoir, imagines her as an old Indian woman, wise and serene, a woman "whose eyelids are a bit heavy," a woman with a "beautiful face, on which age has only inscribed what are called 'expressive wrinkles,' those which underline the smile, the high cheek bones, the crinkling of the eyes." The first book I ever read by Simone de Beauvoir was, as it happens, *The Coming of Age.* So my first encounter with her and thus my first "memory" of her was Simone de Beauvoir at 60, an authoritative, forceful woman whose attitudes toward aging struck me as oddly out of sync with the exemplum of her own life.

An impressive and formidable older woman: that is what Beauvoir grew to be. I am grateful to her legacy to us, as we—whatever our age— imagine for ourselves meaningful links to women older than ourselves. In the end Beauvoir gave us not just her work but her life—as an older and powerful woman.

References

Beauvoir, S. de, 1963. *The Prime of Life,* trans. Richard Howard. New York: Putnam's, p. 653.

Beauvoir, S. de, 1969. *The Age of Discretion,* in *The Woman Destroyed,* trans. Patrick O'Brian. New York. Putnam's.

Beauvoir, S. de, 1972. *The Coming of Age,* trans. Patrick O'Brian. New York: Putnam's.

Butler, R. N., 1972. *The Sunday Star,* Washington, D.C., 28 May, pp. G6 and G6–G7.

Clément, C., 1979. "Peelings of the Real," trans. Elaine Marks. In E. Marks, ed., *Critical Essays on Simone de Beauvoir,* 1987. Boston: Hall, pp. 168–71.

Coles, R., 1972. "Old Age." *The New Yorker,* 19 Aug., p. 68.

Jardine, A., 1979. "Interview with Simone de Beauvoir." *Signs* 5(2): 224–36.

A Personal Journey of Aging

The Spiritual Dimension

Mel Kimble

A t a certain point, one's perceptions of aging become intertwined with perceptions of oneself. In the experience of aging, my credentials get better every day! As a pastoral theologian, I live in a creative tension between the established dogma and practice of my personal faith, on the one hand, and the more generic, encompassing spiritual dimension that is presented here without any primary or specific religious connotation, on the other hand. The spiritual dimension is the energy within that strives for meaning and purpose. It is the unifying and integrating dimension of being that includes the experience of transcendence and the *mysterium tremendum fascinans*, the mystery that is at once overwhelming and fascinating, that renders my existence significant and meaningful in the here and now. It is also a mystery in that it is unmeasurable, unprovable, and lacks universal definition.

A review of my personal history reveals a journey of aging punctuated by a number of milestones that I regard as spiritually significant. I am these life experiences old! They made me what I am. They include my faith commitment and choice of vocation and life partner, as well as other experiences and commitments that have shaped and altered my life at all levels.

Samuel Johnson once remarked that "a hanging has a way of focusing the mind." So does a diagnosis of cancer, especially if it is of the more lethal variety like malignant melanoma. Some ten years ago I had

39

such a diagnosis, followed by major surgery and a grim prognosis. As healing miraculously took place in my body and the cancer went into apparent remission, I felt like Abraham Maslow, who described the time after his first heart attack as his "post-mortem life." So with me; every day was now a bonus, and every person in my life more precious and valued. I began to understand what Paul Tillich meant by the phrase, "the eternal now." Life, faith, and grace seemed to break into my life with greater intensity and sharper focus than ever before. With a greater awareness of my finitude and mortality, time and its passing took on deeper meaning. I was learning and experiencing the difference between *chronos*, calendar time, and *kairos*, eschatological time that involves my ultimate destiny. Both have meaning and value, and are interwoven into my life in a unifying whole.

During this period, my personal faith orientation and commitments were of particular importance. The salvific symbols and rites of my faith tradition and praxis provided powerful sources of meaning in formulating the existential order of my life at this anxious time. Keeping the door open to the transcendent was crucial for me. This meant putting myself in positions and places where such transcendent experiences could break through. Organ concerts that included music of Bach and Langlais were particularly poignant and soul stirring. Even sunrises and sunsets as well as full moons were events not to be missed, especially sunsets shared with loved ones.

C. G. Jung's observation, "That which youth found and had to find outside of itself, in the second half of life must be found within," has become increasingly true for me in my personal journey of aging. Disciplined meditation and prayer have taken on freshness and are experienced as energizing and renewing. Priorities in lifestyle and use of time have been altered and rearranged. All of this is happening in the midst of my own continuous aging process. But with a difference. I am learning what Viktor Frankl has stressed concerning the need to keep the door open between immanence and transcendence.

My spirituality, however, does not exist in some holy haze of isolation, but in relationship and connectiveness, especially with my family and faith community. Special and unique family rituals, for example, have been introduced and have evolved into symbolic and supportive ways of coping with transitions and crises in a universe that is saturated with a blessed ambiguity. The humor and craziness that at times characterize family festive occasions also keep us human and affectionately bonded at many levels, included the spiritual.

The meaning of time and its passing has changed for me. Time past is now more valued. Viktor Frankl maintains that "nothing and nobody can deprive us of what we have safely delivered and deposited in the past." For me, the passing of time is now not erosion but accumulation. The baggage of memories and experiences I now carry on my journey is more complete and full but, suprisingly, not burdensome. I find myself engaged in more reflection and teasing out of meanings of my life from the "storehouse of the past." A configuration, a mosaic of meanings, begins to take shape and leads me forward into the present and to the very precipice of the future. I have discovered that my basic faith in an Ultimate Being who has brought me to the present can be trusted as I face the uncertain and shadowy future.

My journey of aging has more recently taken on a quality that I find somewhat puzzling but intriguing. It is a subtle but discernible movement toward androgyny, and it has some complementary parallels in my wife, JoAnne. It has its roots, as I can now more readily detect, in earlier stages of my life, but it was often blocked or stifled by more repressive roles and prescribed patterns. This melding of masculine and feminine sensitivities has broadened my perception of and response to life as androgynous qualities have emerged and express themselves more spontaneously. It seems that this phenomenon is related to a more holistic expression and formation of my more authentic humanness that includes the spiritual dimension, and I will be interested to continue to track it in the unfolding years of my adult life.

A physician friend of mine contends that there are at least two times in life when persons ought to be required to go off on a retreat and reflect on the meaning of their lives. One, he suggests, is when we choose our vocation; the other is in older adulthood as we get closer to retirement and experience more poignantly the narrowing boundaries of our lives. I have not yet reached the stage of retirement, but I have begun to experience more and more the narrowing boundaries. In my spiritual journey of aging, I have also come to know myself as an indissoluble amalgam of shadow and light, angelic and demonic, in the paradoxical unity of contraries that constitute my essential humanness. As I age, I have become more fully aware of a centripetal spiritual energy that centers and grounds my life and prevails over the centrifugal divisive forces that are ever present, working to spin out and scatter the fragments of my life. It is this power or dimension, rooted in a trust in an Ultimate Being, that enables me to live life at every stage of the life cycle *sub specie aeternitatis,* under the aspect of eternity.

Varieties of Images and Perceptions

Cultural Lags in Social Perceptions of the Aged

Douglas E. Crews

During the final decades of the twentieth century, the elderly have become an increasingly numerous and visible component of the population in many societies. The aged represent a large and expanding proportion of the world's developed societies and are increasing rapidly in many developing and more traditional societies of the globe (Brody, 1989; Kinsella and Suzman, 1992). Total numbers of elderly are much greater in developing nations; however, this increase in numbers of elderly is currently overshadowed by more rapid increases in youthful cohorts (Crews, 1985, 1990a). Both trends have followed massive and rapid reductions in mortality resulting from improved biomedical technologies and public health activities designed to reduce infectious diseases, improve nutrition, and provide safe, healthy environments for infants and children. These health and population trends are expected to continue through at least the twenty-first century (Manton and Tolley, 1991).

Such demographic realignments of age cohorts were originally hypothesized to include declines in the status of the elderly, generational competition over scarce resources, and myriad other social phenomena (Cowgill, 1974; Cowgill and Holmes, 1972). The actual extent of these anticipated consequences has been difficult to document (Eisdorfer, 1981), and the original "modernization theory of aging" has been greatly modified (Cowgill, 1974, 1986). Still, various aspects of these changes have likely produced data offering glimpses of future sociocultural developments that might be anticipated in some populations. Available demographic data allow reconstructions of population structures for some populations (Crews and Smith-Ozeran, 1992). Examination of previous and present sociocultural beliefs enables us to define present, and reconstruct earlier, attitudes toward aging and to estimate the aged life stage. Together, these data may allow quantitative conceptualization of being "aged" or "old" in various societies. Such constructs may be examined to determine whether sociocultural definitions of "old age" have lagged behind biomedical changes leading to continued high physiological and mental function during the seventh, eighth, and even ninth decades of life in many societies. These constructs may allow us to answer questions like the following: Have sociocultural definitions of old age changed in response to new patterns of health and longevity? What factors have been correlates of current attitudes toward the elderly in various populations?

Large cohort trends in survivorship and longevity have been revealed by research in medical and population demography of the U.S. population. Even survivors of chronic disease hospitalizations tend to be older during recent decades. People are living longer and are more healthy at later decades of life than previously (Guralnik, 1991; Kaplan, 1991; Verbrugge, 1991). This trend has been more or less verified across populations (Crews, 1985, 1990b; Stout and Crawford, 1988; Vaupel, 1988; Manton, 1986; Fries, 1988; Olshansky et al., 1991; Wallace and Lemke, 1991).

Cultural definitions of old age developed during earlier periods were related to the prevailing patterns of declining physical and mental functioning. Among the aged, most observable functional capabilities and indicators of health have undergone considerable improvement. This has occurred in response to ecologically altered circumstances of decreased childhood mortality and morbidity, reduced environmental stress, and improved nutrition. It is questionable whether definitions of old age have kept pace with these changes, remained static, or lagged behind.

The purpose of this article is to examine whether scientific and social thinking about long-livedness can profitably be viewed as a problem—described by Weiss (1981) as "cultural lag"—in cultural evolution. Western European cultural definitions of old age were developed when lifespans averaged as little as 30 years. At that time, living 50 years was seen as an exceptional achievement even for royalty (who presumably had the best food and nurturing), and living to age 65 was very extraordinary. For example, of the 11 children of Edward III who survived childbirth, all died of natural causes before reaching age 60, most of them much younger. Thus, not so many years ago, under the Social Security Act of 1935, age 65 was selected for the commencement of retirement and the beginning of old age benefits. Life expectancy in the United States today averages around 75 years. Living to 65 is no longer remarkable, and forced retirement at age 65 has recently become an anachronism outlawed by federal statutes.

Precise and utilitarian definitions of the aged and aging are required for scientific research on aging, formulas for pension benefits, and clinical practice. To understand patterns of aging and age-related disability, chronological age alone is a poor proxy for the study or measurement of aging and senescence. Redefinitions of these concepts have not been widely accepted, however, nor are they of universal utility. Biological and functional age estimates to place relative age in a physiological framework have been explored (Borkan and Norris, 1980), and new conceptualizations such as the "oldest old" (those aged 85 and older) have been developed in attempts to continue to group persons over age 65 in a meaningful way (Suzman and Riley, 1985). This latter method, however, does not differentiate among persons of similar age but different capabilities. Furthermore, even these concepts fail to explain societal expectations that persons of chronological age over 65 are old even when their biological age is 50 and that the vital elderly to be found above age 65 are considered exceptions to the rule. Yet, today's reality is that over 80 percent of U. S. citizens live sufficiently long to receive Social Security benefits (Crews, 1990b).

Such trends toward longer survival are occurring worldwide. This chapter is directed toward (1) examining such demographic trends among aged Samoans, relating observed trends to sociocultural quantification of old age, and (2) exploring possible reasons why young, middle-aged, and older adult Samoans reported variable support for several traditional Samoan customs. The general discussion that follows the specific data from Samoa attempts to link biomedical trends in health and observed cultural responses in a coherent biosocial model of cultural lags in the definition of elders. Links are established between the Samoan experience and similar trends in more cosmopolitan settings like the United States and Great Britain.

47

DEMOGRAPHIC TRENDS

We have extensively examined 1920 through 1989 mortality and census data from the territory of American Samoa (Crews, 1985, 1989, 1990b; Crews and Smith-Ozeran, 1992). These accumulated demographic and voluminous ethnographic data documenting sociocultural trends toward modernization and changing perceptions of aging and the aged (Holmes and Rhodes, 1983; Holmes, 1974; Rhodes, 1981) have been used to explore relationships between demographic trends of increased survivorship and perceptions of old age (*matua*) among American Samoans. Results obtained indicate striking incongruity between sociocultural perceptions and demographic indicators of *matua* during this period of rapid cultural change (Crews and Smith-Ozeran, 1992). By the 1980s, 64 percent of American Samoans survived past age 50, and 40 percent past age 65. Thus, *matua* as defined in 1976 would be applied to 34 percent of Samoans in the 1970s and forty percent in the 1980s. As defined in 1962, *matua* would have applied to 53 percent of people in the 1970s and 64 percent in the 1980s at sometime during their lives. Undoubtedly, this was not a reflection of the realities of life in American Samoa during these periods, but may have reflected retention of earlier cultural beliefs.

Retention of "outdated" definitions of *matua* among Samoans, that is, concepts based primarily on prior cultural experiences no longer congruent with new realities of extended life and healthy lifespans, can be described as "cultural lags." Change in ages generally reported as *matua* between 1962 and 1976 by American Samoans imply that sociocultural definitions of *matua* were likely responding to improved survivorship, health, and physiological functioning of the elderly (Crews, 1989; Crews and Smith-Ozeran, 1992). Still, a response lag between the cultural definition of old age and these new realities is apparent. This type of "cultural lag" is likely to be found in other populations where trends in life expectancy, changing demographic patterns, and improvements in healthcare are outpacing sociocultural definitions of aging (see Smyer and Crews, 1985; Crews, in press). Weiss (1981) defined such lags in cultural definitions of the aged in comparison to the reality of life expectancies of seven and eight decades as a problem in cultural evolution. Some similar lags may be found among most populations, including our own.

For example, in 1935, when the United States established the Social Security Administration, only 15 percent of the population lived to age 65 or older. During the five decades since, the percentage of the U.S. population surviving to age 65 and over has increased steadily—today about 80 percent survive past age 65. Yet, there has been no associated change in the age at which persons receive Social Security benefits nor in our accepted chronological definition of old age during this period (Suzman and Riley, 1985). This illustrates a problem in the sociocultural evolution of our definitions of old age—a cultural lag in defining the elderly. It probably also reflects a social reality that sociocultural patterns change only as those with the greatest investments in the prevailing system leave the system through attrition, eliminating the need to maintain the previous definitions (Smyer and Crews, 1985).

It appears that a cultural lag is occurring in Samoan definitions of *matua*. At least two major changes are influencing this lag. For one, older individuals raised in the traditions of *fa'asamoa* (the Samoan way) continue to live these traditions and expect from others (young adults) close conformity to *fa'asamoa*. Perhaps the cultural lag is partly the result of elders attempting to retain their traditional roles and prerogatives (Crews and Baker, 1982)—attempts that elders often perceive as successful. Second, middle-aged and young adults are often finding larger personal rewards in new economic markets while at the same time retaining a foothold in the traditional system, apparently to buffer possible setbacks in a precarious labor market. Thus, the observed cultural lags in redefining *matua* may serve both older and younger cohorts, the elderly by allowing them to reap the benefits of long-term investments in the traditional cultural system, and the working age adults by providing a stable cultural refuge in times of stress. Thus, the first factor in the development of a cultural lag in Samoa may be stability of the definition of *matua* within the traditional culture. A second more subtle factor influencing the cultural lag may be a reluctance on the part of those fully participating in the introduced, but foreign, culture of economic and technological modernization to completely forgo *fa'asamoa* and the traditional system of rewards and prerogatives. In this respect, both generations may be cooperating more to retain traditional cultural values than responses to the survey cited by Crews and Baker (1982) may indicate. A majority of older and younger respondents alike responded that Samoan customs are a good

49

thing. They disagreed on the principles of *matai* (Samoan family chiefs) rule and contributing to support of the *aiga* (the Samoan extended family)—fairly onerous impositions for individuals participating in a culture of individual freedom and individual recompense for personal labors while at work.

What does all this mean for practitioners in industrialized populations like the United States and Great Britain? For one, caregivers, clinicians, nurses, and allied health workers are likely to have frequent encounters with aged persons of different ethnic groups who, although participating in the dominant culture system and being perceived within the context of the dominant culture's lags, are experiencing their own culturally specific lags. (See Galanti, 1991, for several anecdotes of this type of phenomenon.) This situation is likely to be particularly acute in places like the United States with its large mix of ethnic groups—African, Hispanic, Asian, Pacific Islander, European, and Native Americans—and Great Britain with its mix of Afro-Caribbeans, Asians, English, Irish, Welsh, and Scottish. Traditional ethnic patterns and cultural concepts of aging and age-appropriate health, personal, and social behaviors are likely to be largely incongruent not only with the mainstream culture, but also with current patterns of morbidity, mortality, and survivorship within the ethnic group. Thus, individuals from U.S. cultures outside the mainstream are likely to be at double jeopardy because of the medicalization of aging here. This view has been proposed by recent theorists of aging among ethnic minorities for sociocultural stress and health. (See Markides and Mindel, 1987, for a review of minority theories of aging.)

Cultural lags do not occur only in traditional societies experiencing rapid economic and technological modernization. Members of mainstream cultural groups also experience such lags, although they may be less pronounced than those of developing cultures. One example is the retention of age 65 as the mandatory retirement age throughout our own society until recently, when such age discrimination was outlawed by federal statute. Before the passage of this law, however, the majority of the U.S. population that was of working force age in 1935, and who contributed to the early Social Security fund, were already well beyond retirement age; actually, most are now older than the present-day average life expectancy or are already deceased. The implication that this cultural lag was maintained as long as it benefited those who had invested in the original (read traditional) system is obvious and perhaps worth further investigation.

Such instances of generational conflict do not occur when elders are inactive and dependent upon others to complete activities of life. Rather, conflict occurs when elders tend to outlive their expected life-spans, retain their vigor, and live independent lives that cultural patterns have not previously evolved to accommodate. Other examples of such cultural lags abound in European ethnic traditions: While primogeniture and the retention of family lands by the oldest male until his demise may have worked well in certain cases, British history and literature are replete with conflicts between aging sons and sires. William the Conqueror was one of several kings who fought a civil war against his own eldest son. Any analysis of literary fiction and biographies from any land will reveal similar generational conflicts that serve to illustrate cultural lags in defining the aged and their place in changing societies.

There is a need to understand not only *emic* (internal to a culture) and *etic* (external viewpoint on cultural phenomenon) perspectives on aging, but also *individualistic* perceptions of aging and being aged. Individual perceptions and patterns of aging are probably more variable than are ideal concepts of aging. Since all biological and physiological measurements show increased variation with increasing age, it stands to reason that beliefs and individual responses to aging will also be highly variable. One person's cultural lag may be another's cultural reality. All residents of the United States or their ancestors, except Native Americans, arrived here from a specific external culture and all carry with them aspects of their cultural history that are molded by current cultural circumstances. There are several aspects of current cultural circumstances that we all share: reduced infant mortality, improved health and survivorship, and longer lives than have ever previously been attained by the vast majority of humans. These trends are superimposed on traditional family and individual expectations and may lead to discontinuities between current realities and outmoded definitions of life stages. When such discontinuities arise, they give the appearance of lags in cultural evolution. It may be that some age cohorts, either consciously or unconsciously, attempt to retain traditional patterns of age relations because they have already invested most of their lives in the traditional system. As those with large previous and perhaps current investments succumb to natural processes of attrition, sociocultural pressures release old cultural lags only to expose new patterns of cultural lags as younger cohorts age. However, these should themselves show a degree of lag or incongruity with present circumstances as those experiencing them may have large investments in the current cultural system and its rewards.

Acknowledgments

The author wishes to thank Robert Cope for his expert typing assistance and for providing several historical notes as examples for concepts developed in this presentation, and Dena Shenk for her useful suggestions and review of an earlier draft of this manuscript.

References

Borkan, G. A., and Norris, A. H., 1980. "Assessment of Biological Age Using a Profile of Physical Parameters." *Journal of Gerontology* 35: 177–84.

Brody, J. A., 1989. "Toward Quantifying the Health of the Elderly." *American Journal of Public Health* 79: 685–86.

Cowgill, D. O., 1974. "Aging and Modernization: A Revision of Theory." In J. Gubrium, ed., *Late Life: Communities and Environment Policy*. Springfield, Ill.: Charles C. Thomas.

Cowgill, D. O., 1986. *Aging Around the World*. Belmont, Calif.: Wadsworth.

Cowgill, D. O., and Holmes, L. D., 1972, eds. *Aging and Modernization*. New York: Appleton-Century-Crofts.

Crews, D. E., 1985. "Mortality, Survivorship and Longevity in American Samoa 1950–1981." Ph.D. diss. The Pennsylvania State University.

Crews, D. E., 1989. "Cause-specific Mortality, Life Expectancy, and Debilitation in Aging Polynesians." *American Journal of Human Biology* 1: 347–53.

Crews, D. E., 1990a. "Anthropological Issues in Biological Gerontology." In R. L. Rubinstein, ed., *Anthropology and Aging: Comprehensive Reviews*. Dordrecht, The Netherlands: D. Reidel, pp. 11–38.

Crews, D. E., 1990b. "Multiple Causes of Death, Chronic Diseases, and Aging." *Collegium Anthropologicum* 14: 197–204.

Crews, D. E., in press. "Biological Anthropology of Human Aging: New

Directions in Aging Research." *Annual Review of Anthropology* 22.

Crews, D. E., and Baker, T. S., 1982. "Aging and Culture Change in Samoa: A Comparison of Traditional and Modern Life-Styles." *Gerontologist* 22: 260–61 (Abstract). Full manuscript available on request.

Crews, D. E,. and Smith-Ozeran, J. E., 1992. "Historical Demographic and Epidemiological Studies of Aging in American Samoans." *American Journal of Human Biology* 4(1):9–16.

Eisdorfer, C., 1981. Foreword. In P. T. Amoss and S. Harrell, eds., *Other Ways of Growing Old: Anthropological Perspectives.* Stanford, Calif.: Stanford University Press.

Fries, J. F., 1988. "Aging, Illness, and Health Policy:Implications of the Compression of Morbidity." *Perspectives in Biological Medicine* 31: 407–28.

Galanti, G. A., 1991. *Caring for Patients from Different Cultures: Case Studies from American Hospitals.* Philadelphia: University of Pennsylvania Press.

Guralnik, J. M., 1991. "Prospects for the Compression of Morbidity: The Challenge Posed by Increasing Disability in the Years Prior to Death." *Journal of Aging Health* 3(2): 138–54.

Holmes, L. D., 1974. *Samoan Village.* New York: Holt, Rinehart and Winston.

Holmes, L. D., and Rhodes, E. C., 1983. "Aging and Change in Samoa." In J. Sokolovsky, ed., *Growing Old in Different Societies: Cross-Cultural Perspectives.* Belmont, Calif.: Wadsworth, pp. 119–29.

Kaplan, G. A., 1991. "Epidemiologic Observations on the Compression of Mortality: Evidence from the Alameda County Study." *Journal of Aging Health* 3(2): 155–71.

Kinsella, K., and Suzman, R., 1992. "Demographic Dimensions of Population Aging in Developing Countries." *American Journal of Human Biology* 4(1): 3–8.

Manton, K. G., 1986. "Past and Future Life Expectancy Increases at Later Ages: Their Implications for the Linkage of Chronic Morbidity, Disability, and Mortality." *Journal of Gerontology* 41: 672–81.

Manton, K. G., and Tolley, H. D., 1991. "Rectangularization of the Survival Curve: Implications of an Ill-Posed Question." *Journal of Aging Health* 3(2): 172–93.

Markides, K. S., and Mindel, C. H., 1987. *Ethnicity and Aging.* Newbury Park, Calif.: Sage.

Olshansky, S. J., et al., 1991. "Trading Off Longer Life for Worsening Health: The Expansion of Morbidity Hypothesis." *Journal of Aging Health* 3(2): 194–216.

Rhodes, E. C., 1981. "Aging and Modernization in Three Samoan Communities." Ph.D. diss. Lawrence, Kans.: University of Kansas.

Smyer, M. A., and Crews, D. E., 1985. "'Developmental' Intervention and Aging: Demographic and Economic Change as a Context for Intervention." In D. A. Kleiber and M. L. Maehr, eds., *Advances in Motivation and Achievement: Motivation and Adulthood.* Greenwich, Conn.: JAI Press.

Stout, R. W., and Crawford, V., 1988. "Active Life Expectancy and Terminal Dependency: Trends in Long-Term Geriatric Care over 33 Years." *Lancet* (Feb.): 281–83.

Suzman, R., and Riley, N. W., 1985. "Introducing the 'Oldest Old.'" *Milbank Memorial Fund Quarterly* 63: 177–86.

Vaupel, J. W., 1988. "Inherited Frailty and Longevity." *Demography* 25: 277–87.

Verbrugge, L., 1991. "Survival Curves, Prevalence Rates, and Dark Matters Therein." *Journal of Aging Health* 3(2): 217–36.

Wallace, R. B., and Lemke, J. H., 1991. "The Compression of Comorbidity." *Journal of Aging Health* 3(2): 237–46.

Weiss, K. M., 1981. "Evolutionary Perspectives on Human Aging." In P. T. Amoss and S. Harrell, eds., *Other Ways of Growing Old: Anthropological Perspectives.* Stanford, Calif.: Stanford University Press.

Images of Old Age in America 1790–1970—After a Second Look

W. Andrew Achenbaum

Whatever new object we see, we perceive to be only a new version of our familiar experience, and we set about translating it at once into our parallel facts. We have thereby our vocabulary.

—Ralph Waldo Emerson
"Art and Criticism"

There are close connections, Ralph Waldo Emerson notes, among seeing, thinking, and communicating. On the surface, this is a simple story about crossing boundaries from the printed word to the visual image: A historian (myself) and an art librarian (Peg Kusnerz) in 1976 were given six months to produce an exhibit of *Images of Old Age in America,* 1790 to the Present, which would suggest the cultural-historical factors that shaped the meanings and experiences of old age. We agreed on two lithographs—"The Life and Age of Man/Woman" and "Stages of a Man's/Woman's Life from the Cradle to the Grave," which were published by James Baille in 1848 (Figs. 7.1 and 7.2). We then divided the presentation into three parts. The first section (1790–1864) accentuated the positive, the second (1865–1934) the negative, the third (1935–ca. 1976) blended the first two (Achenbaum and Kusnerz, 1978, p. 2).

The Smithsonian Institution Traveling Exhibition Services took *Images* to colleges, banks, zoos, art galleries. The exhibit hung at the 1981 White House Conference on Aging; the catalog won several awards, suggesting an impact beyond our wildest expectations. Now, it seems appropriate to ask how well we *really* accomplished our objectives. Did we present images sufficiently rich in composition and content to show the diversity of earlier generations of older Americans? Are better resources available? Have our perceptions of historical realities greatly changed since 1976?

Figure 7.1. "The Life and Age of Man. Stages of a Man's Life from the Cradle to the Grave." James Baille, 1848. Library of Congress.

Figure 7.2. "The Life and Age of Woman. Stages of a Woman's Life from the Cradle to the Grave." James Baille, 1848. Library of Congress.

56

CONTENT

"Rather than attributing divergent conceptions of older people's worth to the March of Progress or the Loss of Virtue, we tried to indicate that they represent differences in kind rather than quality of values operating in society over time." We wanted to smash "simplistic" and "simpleminded" images of what old age was like in the past. As a corollary, we also thought it possible to create images that would facilitate our desire for "older men and women—and ultimately ourselves—to play roles in society that ensure meaning and dignity to their lives" (Achenbaum and Kusnerz, 1978, p. viii).

There were many questions about "diversity"; we were concerned that women, Blacks, Asians, Native Americans, and other groups were sufficiently represented in the exhibit. We did not maintain a quota system; some simple counts are revealing.

We used 34 images to cover the period between 1790 and 1864. Two-thirds came from the 1840s and 1850s. Women are in 10 images, couples in two. Blacks are in two photographs; there is a pencil drawing of Pagh-Paght-sem-i-am, a Native American named "Woman of Good Sense." Six graphics stress intergenerational themes—although we discarded literally hundreds of sentimental renditions of the bonds between young and old. Six pictures portrayed American heroes (including Benjamin Franklin and Johnny Appleseed).

I am struck, in retrospect, by several interesting features. Canes are prominent icons in six graphics, yet only three images executed between 1790 and 1864 emphasized death or the risks of dependency in late life. Furthermore, the faces of older Americans in the first section are remarkably ebullient, regardless of their social condition or economic status. Even the "hermit who lived upwards of 200 years" looks none the worse for wear after spending most of his life in a dank cave.

The 30 graphics used in the second section convey a darker image. Nearly a third of the pictures accentuate unflattering features of living (too) long, although curiously, there are *no* pictures of the old-old in this part! Elderly people are shown among the other deserving poor in an almshouse, at the Freedman's Bureau, or claiming veterans benefits. Only one famous person (Henry Wadsworth Longfellow) is represented here. Among the ordinary citizens portrayed are five couples, three older people in the company of younger people, six women, two Blacks, one Native American, and one Asian.

Thanks to photographs taken for the Farm Security Agency in the latter part of the 1930s, we had no difficulty accentuating old-old diversity in the "contemporary" section, with photographs of a Texas Mexican husband and wife, Mennonite farmers, a Latina, the wife of a migrant worker in California, a male ex-slave in Georgia, and a Spanish-American farmer. The very old once again seem slighted, represented only by an ex-slave and Imogen Cunningham's picture of her father at 90. Nonetheless, endorsing the "new" social history then in vogue, there are many images of ordinary people shopping, dancing, learning, and protesting.

Women constitute about a third of the images in all sections, but in the last part, by design, large numbers are shown together sitting on benches—with men conspicuously absent. We wanted to show the widening gender gap. But despite our sensitivity to intergenerational issues, there is only one picture of a child walking with her grandfather. Did we take too literally the gerontologic notion, fashionable in the 1970s, that age cohorts were becoming increasingly segregated?

Were Peg Kusnerz and I to revise *Images of Old Age in America*, we would still want to stress the heterogeneity of elderly Americans, accentuating the theme of "pluralism" even more forcibly in five ways:

1. The introductory section would be longer, in order to underscore the importance of perduring themes of old age in Western civilization over the centuries. Prototypes for the first two visuals can be traced back to fifteenth century Augsburg. Even though renditions of this motif of "rise and decline" over the human life course have persisted for nearly four centuries, viewers need to appreciate that there have always been many ways to conceptualize aging: There were at least 16 different versions of the "steps of the ages" popular in nineteenth century France alone (Achenbaum and Kusnerz, 1978, p. 71). Patrick McKee and Heta Kauppinen selected 116 portraits of age from Western art that "express the challenges, satisfactions, sorrows, and joys in the human experience of growing old" (1987, p. 13). J. A. Burrow's *The Ages of Man* (1986) concentrates on contravarieties in medieval iconography. Mary Dove (1986) offers an alternative interpretation of the same material, stressing the ambiguity inherent in notions that any particular age in life is the "perfect" age.

By incorporating these works, it would be possible to begin, not end, with the notion that various artists at divergent stages of life have stressed different features at distinct stages of life. Artists the same age, moreover, often have disagreed in their conceptions of the journey of life. The elderly themselves face life's finitude differently. It is a fruitless distortion to invoke a single motif to capture the variegated images of late life.

2. *The gender-specific themes identified in the two Introductory graphics would be accentuated, and then the theme carried out more systematically in the catalog.* In my "Afterword" (Achenbaum and Kusnerz, 1982, p. ix), I noted some important gender-specific variations in the first two graphics. The officer in his prime at 50 still appeared vigorous 20 years later. In contrast, by the sixth decade, the burdens of caregiving appear to have drained the woman of her vitality. Then the pattern seems to reverse in later years: the man "retires" at 70 to increasing obsolescence; the woman is not depicted as a "useless cumberer" until 90.

Current research (Gilligan, 1982; Gutmann, 1987) supports several presuppositions embedded in these historical images. Carol Gilligan (1982) argues that men and women think and speak "in a different voice." I would invoke Nancy Cott's *Bonds of Womanhood* (1971) and Terri Premo's *Winter Friends* (1989) to underscore the point that women in the early years of the Republic developed ties with other women that sustained and nurtured them over the interconnected lives. Greater reference should be made to women's roles as caregivers and as widows.

In retrospect, I wish we had not been so hasty in passing over an irenic photograph of Maggie Kuhn: Showing the feisty convener of the Gray Panthers as reflective and content might have underlined the complexity of sentiments about growing older within each of us as we age.

3. *The "political" content of images of old age often affects how we see the elderly's assets, liabilities, contributions, and circumstances.* "Pluralism" is a political term, not merely a sociological construct. Accordingly, we should have acknowledged that norms and conventions often determine the ways that the content in the images we selected was expressed. *The Gallery of Illustrious Americans* by Mathew Brady (1850), for instance, offered a dozen daguerreotypes of "representative" older men, including two mediocre presidents (Zachary Taylor and Millard Fillmore).

We also want to try to capture the degradation and horrors of slavery through a cache of photographs discovered recently. In 1850 Louis Agassiz, a distinguished Harvard professor of natural science, commissioned J. T. Zealy, a South Carolina daguerreotypist, to take pictures of the faces and bodies of black slaves. Rather than honor the hoary heads of "illustrious," "representative" citizens, the subjects of Zealy's photographs stand naked. They are specimens, "types," exhibited for the advancement of science. "The Zealy pictures reveal the social convention which ranks Blacks as inferior beings, which violates civilized decorum, which strips men and women of the right to cover their genitalia" (Trachtenberg, 1989, p. 56). The sullen looks, the pain, the scars on older women's sagging breasts and aging men's sunken chests, are haunting. Such traits also characterize late nineteenth-century photographs of the elderly sick, which presumably also were taken for "scientific" purposes. Such images attest to the extent to which objectivity dehumanizes.

4. More attention should have been paid to Latinos and Native Americans in the Southwest. Most of the graphics in *Images of Old Age* dealt with subjects who live(d) east of the Mississippi. (To be sure, a comparable Eastern (northern) urban bias runs through most of the historical literature on old age in the United States.) As a result the extent of the diversity that has long existed among the people who settled in the Plains and the American Southwest is not fully evident here. Too bad that Peg and I did not know that the child psychiatrist Robert Coles and the photographer Alex Harris had published a book about *The Old Ones of New Mexico*. "The people are strong, proud, vigorous, independent. They are of 'Spanish' descent, yet can be called 'old-line' Americans," Coles reports. "Others from the Anglo world might consider them aloof, old-fashioned, superstitious, all too set in their ways. They look upon themselves quite differently; they hold to certain values and assumptions, and, God willing, they will not forsake them" (Coles and Harris, 1973, pp. xii-xiii). We also would want to include pictures and graphics about the Native Americans and Mormons who interact(ed) with Spanish-speaking peoples in the Southwest. For instance, a 1974 acrylic entitled "Emergence" by Hopi artist Dawakema-Milland Lomakema might be used, not only to contrast the "stages of life" graphics in the "Introduction," but also to show a highly distinctive conception of time, one not linear but cumulative (Boyle and Morriss, 1987).

5. That time passes within the country of the old must be underlined. Despite the attention paid in *Images of Old Age* to the old-old in the nineteenth century, with its daguerreotypes of centenarians, this exhibit does not stress that Americans now expect to live longer than ever before, that two-thirds of all gains in life expectancy in the world have been made since 1900. Nor did we indicate that with added years has come a greater incidence of chronicity, which puts strains on the country's healthcare system.

We might have emphasized some of the tragedies associated with the medicalization and bureaucratization of age—ranging from the prolongation of vegetable-like existence through heroic interventions to the impoverishment of middle-class citizens so that they qualify for Medicaid while in nursing homes.

METHOD

In her comments in the 1982 "Afterword" (Achenbaum and Kusnerz, 1982, p. x), Peg Kusnerz stated what friends and critics had already told us privately: "I believe the weakest section of the book is part three (1935–present)." Had Kusnerz and I embarked on this project a few years later, we would have been able to take advantage of the outpouring of monographs and basic reference works that deal with humanistic perspectives on aging (Polisar et al., 1988). We might have included "stills" from motion pictures and television. Robert Yahnke's survey of films (1988) would be the starting point for analyzing the incidence of older people in cinema, as well as how aging actors and actresses must adapt their personae in the latter stages of their careers. Tracing views of aging on television since the 1950s would have added much to what we know about images in postwar America. Older people are among the most important consumers of network programming, both in terms of numbers of hours per day they watch programs as well as in terms of the companionship they derive from "friends" on the screen (Davis and Davis, 1985).

Even without additions from television or films, better selections might have broadened the range of imagery in the third part. Archibald MacLeish's *Land of the Free* (1938) is "a book of photographs illustrated by a poem" (p. 89). Roughly an eighth of the photographs, mostly taken for the Resettlement Administration, feature elderly subjects—including a hauntingly beautiful pair of wrinkled hands. Picture 22 in Walker Evans's *American Photographs*, "An Alabama Tenant Family Singing Hymns" (1936), shows a couple in their 30s holding a dog-eared hymnal. Their daughter, mouth closed, looks off vacantly. The mother of one of the parents keeps her distance from the couple; eyes closed, she sings from memory. There is nothing dramatic here, but in Lincoln Kirstein's words, Evans so powerfully conveys "the effect of circumstances on familiar specimens" (Evans, 1938, p. 197) that it makes manifest the strength as well as the attenuation in intergenerational bonds. Powerful photographs of well-known elderly people that

61

appeared in *Life* merit consideration. Yet a systematic survey of the magazine suggests that, until recently, the elderly rarely appeared in the magazine's pages (Poit, 1990). Nor were the editors of *Life* alone in ignoring or stereotyping the old. It is remarkable that there is not one memorable picture of the aged in Robert Frank's *The Americans* (1958), arguably the best collection of photographs published during the decade. Much of the art of presenting images of old age becomes a matter of critical interpretation.

INTERPRETATION

On balance, *Images of Old Age in America* did succeed in indicating changes in values attributed to old age and in the ways that the elderly have lived during the past two centuries, but the tripartite division is too neat. The presentation would have been more compelling, in my view, had we made more of an effort to portray aging over time as a dynamic, variegated process. Were Peg and I to update *Images of Old Age*, we would want to underline our interpretation of "time" as a central element (factually and metaphorically) of aging.

One way to underline themes in the antebellum and contemporary periods of U.S. history would be to compare the ways that a well-known artist from each era interpreted the human life course. The first section of Images now ends with a copy of Smillie's 1849 engraving of Thomas Cole's "Old Age" (1849), which was one of four paintings Cole did to convey his sense of the "Voyage of Life." In a revised version of *Images of Old Age*, I would reproduce "Childhood," "Youth," and "Middle Age," pointing out some of the obvious motifs. Bright light radiates the promise of youth; darkness, in contrast, shrouds old age except for that stream of light focusing the old mariner's attention to the eternal. The waters become progressively turbulent. The guardian angel who hovered over the innocent child is the one who shows the way in the last act. In the middle pictures, the angel is there, but ignored by the sailor who feels that he is in his prime. Cole's interpretation is meant to be inspirational; as befits his message, he paints on huge canvases.

Jasper Johns's series on the voyage of life, "The Seasons" (1986), would be an apt counterpoint. Cole's protagonist braves the elements; Johns also frames his message in Nature. True to contemporary sensibilities, however, Johns offers a complex, fragmented, chaotic sense of aging. No longer God, but science, offers any promise of stability.

Whereas shadows convey a sense of mystery in the nineteenth-century series, they underscore ambiguity in the later work. As symbolic in composition as Cole, Johns is more eclectic in his idiosyncratic melding of ancient icons and modern motifs. "Where Cole's 'Voyage' is about keeping one's faith and surviving life's trials, Johns's 'Seasons' is about essential questions of identity, change and continuity in our perplexing and foundationless 'post-modern' world," notes the cultural historian Tom Cole (who is no relation to the antebellum painter). "The sense of vision presented by Johns involves the resurrection of the past, the necessity of traditional archetypes to help guide us into our uncertain future" (Cole, 1991; see also Rosenthal, 1988).

Johns's provocative "vocabulary" brings us full circle back to Emerson's epigraph. Johns borrows from tradition to give his viewers images from "our familiar experience" so we can try to make sense of issues so profound, so elusive that we really do not know how to possess them, how to translate them "into our present facts." Johns does not present us with a neat picture: He deftly treats the contingent, uncertain manner in which people must wrestle with historically grounded and universal features of human aging. Jasper Johns's "The Seasons" makes possible a continuing dialogue about aging. This conversation must begin rather than end with an appreciation of the pluralism inherent in the human condition, which affirms various ways of growing older. The dialogue need not rely just on words, but on any form of communication that facilitates insights about aging.

References

Achenbaum, W. A., 1978. *Old Age in the New Land: The American Experience since 1790.* Baltimore, Md.: Johns Hopkins University Press.

Achenbaum, W. A., and Kusnerz, P. A., 1978. *Images of Old Age in America, 1790 to the Present.* Ann Arbor, Mich.: Institute of Gerontology.

Achenbaum, W. A., and Kusnerz, P. A., 1982. *Images of Old Age in America, 1790 to the Present,* rev. ed. Ann Arbor, Mich.: Institute of Gerontology.

Boyle, J. M., and Morriss, J. E., 1987. *The Mirror of Time.* Westport, Conn.: Greenwood Press.

Burrow, J. A., 1986. *The Ages of Man.* Oxford, England: Clarendon Press.

VARIETIES OF IMAGES AND PERCEPTIONS

Callihan, D., 1987. *Setting Limits.* New York: Simon & Schuster.

Cole, T. R., 1991. "Aging, Metaphor, and Meaning." In G. M. Kenyon, J. E. Birren and J. F. Schroots, eds., *Metaphors of Aging in Science and the Humanities.* New York: Springer.

Coles, R., and Harris, A., 1973. *The Old Ones of New Mexico.* Albuquerque, N. Mex.: University of New Mexico Press.

Cott, N., 1971. *Bonds of Womanhood.* New Haven, Conn.: Yale University Press.

Davis, R. H., and Davis, J. A., 1985. *TV's Image of the Elderly.* Lexington, Mass.: Lexington Books.

Dove, M., 1986. *The Perfect Age of Man's Life.* Cambridge: Cambridge University Press.

Evans, W., 1938. *American Photographs.* New York: Museum of Modern Art.

Frank, R., 1958. *The Americans.* New York: Grove Press.

Gilligan, C., 1982. *In a Different Voice.* Cambridge, Mass.: Harvard University Press.

Gutmann, D., 1987. *Powers Reclaimed.* New York: Basic Books.

MacLeish, A., 1938. *Land of the Free.* New York: Harcourt, Brace.

McKee, P., and Kauppinen, H., 1987. *The Art of Aging.* New York: Human Sciences Press.

Poit, K., 1990. "Images of the Elderly through the Eyes of Life." Unpublished seminar paper, University of Michigan.

Polisar, D., et al., 1988. *Where Do We Come From? What Are We? Where Are We Going?* Washington, D.C.: Gerontological Society of America.

Premo, T., 1989. *Winter Friends.* Urbana, Ill.: University of Illinois Press.

Rosenthal, M., 1988. *Jasper Johns: Work since 1974.* Philadelphia: Philadelphia Museum of Art.

Trachtenberg, A., 1989. *Reading American Photographs.* New York: Hill & Wang.

Yahnke, R. E., 1988. *The Great Circle of Life: A Resource Guide to Films on Aging.* Owings Mills, Md.: National Institutes on Health.

Ancient Images of Aging

Did Ageism Exist in Greco-Roman Antiquity?

Judith de Luce

When Virgil describes the entrance to the Underworld in *Aeneid* 6.273–277, he locates old age in the company of the grimmest realities of human experience: grief, care, disease, "sad" old age, fear, hunger, poverty, and death. Whether or not this description reflects the experience of actual Greeks and Romans, it certainly reflects a popular perception of old age in Virgil's time. But does it imply the existence of attitudes in Greco-Roman antiquity that could be called ageist and that could have given rise to discrimination against elders?

I want to explore this question by using Butler's (1989) definition of ageism as "a systematic stereotyping of and discrimination against people because they are old, just as racism and sexism accomplish this with skin color and gender" (p. 139). The study of old age in the ancient world has suffered from a kind of ageism, which scholars are beginning to remedy (Haynes, 1962, 1963; Bertman, 1976; Kebric, 1983; Bremmer, 1987; Falkner and de Luce, 1989, 1992; Garland, 1990). Until recently, classicists had maintained a persistent silence about elders in general, and old women in particular, in part because of the nature of the evidence available, in part because of the narrow perspectives of scholars.

The question, though, is not whether classicists are ageists, but rather whether Greece and Rome practiced discrimination on the basis of age. To date we have no better evidence that elders were disadvantaged than that they were privileged. What we do have is a literary tradition that depicts elders according to a fairly predictable pattern of character traits and behaviors. I propose to explore that tradition here. It remains to be seen whether these traits form a stereotype of the elder.

Greece and Rome were linguistically related and nearly contiguous, but we cannot assume that their cultures were interchangeable. Certainly neither the Greeks nor the Romans believed this. General statements about growing old in Greece do not necessarily apply to Romans as well. I have focused here on evidence primarily from Rome, citing evidence from Greece when it would supplement the picture. Rather than striving for anything like comprehensiveness, I have selected evidence that reveals a broad range of attitudes. This evidence, while far from supporting some facile claim for the relevance of the ancient to the modern world, may suggest legitimate correspondences or continuity between attitudes from classical antiquity to our own time.

Before proceeding, we need to remember what "old" meant in antiquity. Demographic information is uneven at best and does not readily allow for confident interpretation, but in general, women would have been regarded as old after menopause, probably by age 40. Men would have been regarded as old by age 50 (de Luce, 1993). It is harder to estimate how many people in Greece or Rome actually attained old age, but probably less than 1 percent reached the age of 80 (Garland, 1990). Evidence suggests that 70 years was regarded as the usual life span, with the median age of death approximately 35 for women, 45 for men (Hopkins, 1966; Angel, 1972, table 28).

Did the Greeks and Romans systematically discriminate against elders as a group? Perhaps the most provocative evidence we have to suggest that ageism existed in Rome is the enigmatic saying, *sexagenarios de ponte* (60-year-olds from the bridge), which appears to encourage hurling elders from some bridge, presumably one over the Tiber. Ovid does not believe that this is what it means (*Fasti* 5.621), and neither should we. In Rome, voters were marshaled across "bridges" into the polling places. It is more likely that the saying refers to generational antagonism at election time than to some concerted determination on the part of the Romans to dispose of their elders after the age of 60.

In Sparta the Gerousia, the Council of Elders, was a central part of the political structure, but Sparta can hardly be taken as the norm for the rest of Greece. Rome functioned according to the principles of seniority, not gerontocracy, and various social and political institutions provided opportunities for male elders to remain active and influential in Roman life (Plescia, 1976; Van Tassel, 1988). While there may not have been many Romans living into old age, those we know of do not seem to have been barred because of their age from civic life, politics, artistic activity, and so on. Cato the Elder, for example, remained politically active until his death at 85, as did Cicero, who died at 63. We do not find a reluctance to name as emperor men who were no longer young or even middle-aged. A man did not retire from his life-long obligation to serve in the Senate (whose very name derives from the word for old man) until he was 60 or 65, or from jury duty until he was 60. He could retire from military duty at 50. Cato the Elder (*De Senectute* 18.64) says that within the high-ranking College of Augurs, the privilege of speaking first in debate went to the oldest men of that body. This does not suggest systematic discrimination against old men.

Pliny describes influential Roman elders such as Spurinna, 77, in his letters (3.1). Not only does Pliny cherish the opportunity to talk with someone of Spurinna's age, rather like Socrates with Cephalus, but Pliny would model his own old age after that of Spurinna. Spurinna maintained his physical and mental health by exercising his body and his mind. He enjoyed the respect and affection of many and was free of the sexual passions that plague younger men. In fact, Pliny says that while excitement may be an appropriate part of young men's lives, "their elders should lead a quiet and orderly existence; their time of public activity is over...." Spurinna's comfortable, intellectual life may be the exception, however; Pliny also describes a Corinthian bronze he has just bought—an old man with wrinkled skin, thinning hair, hollow chest, and haggard expression. This piece is reminiscent of the Hellenistic figures depicting a desperately thin old woman lugging a pail or a drunken old woman clasping a jug.

Postmenopausal women, while no longer valued for their fecundity, might still exert considerable influence within their families, and while they did not vote or hold office and were thus barred from the political activities that engaged a Cato or a Cicero well into old age, upper-class Roman women were hardly invisible (Hallett, 1984). Tacitus includes portraits of old women who exhibited courage, cunning, and initiative, and Pliny writes about such old women as Ummidia Quadratilla, who remained physically and mentally vigorous until her death at almost 79. He approves of the provisions she made for her grandchildren, especially her grandson, in her will. While Pliny certainly does not think much of her lifestyle, he does approve of her efforts to prevent her grandson from seeing the performances of her resident mime troupe. However, Ummidia Quadratilla may also be an exception. She was a wealthy woman and, as Plato's Cephalus and Cicero's Cato both observe, old age can indeed be more comfortable if you have money. Laws in Athens as well as Rome expected children to care for their aging parents and provided for actions if they did not. These laws remind us of the economic vulnerability of elders in the absence of social services to provide care if the family would not or could not (Schaps, 1979; Falkner and de Luce, 1992).

While our evidence about the private lives of actual Greeks and Romans is uneven at best, literary representations make up a compelling picture of how these cultures regarded growing old. Poetry is particularly useful in this regard because by its very nature it transcends particular instances and therefore can provide a vision of human experience that is not specific to place or time. It was for this reason that Aristotle argued in the *Poetics* that "poetry is something more scientific and serious than history, because poetry tends to give general truths while history gives particular facts" (ix.1–3).

We can begin with Horace. When the poet recommends that writers abide by the principle of *tempestivitas*, or age-grading, so that their characters will be convincing, he perpetuates traditional representations of old men. Like Plato, Cicero, and Plutarch, he does not mention old women. While he describes childhood, adolescence, and maturity in a fairly even-handed way, when he turns to old age he resorts to wholly negative characteristics:

> *And men grown old suffer,*
> *Rich but afraid to spend, not daring to eat,*
> *Sick of living but sicker at death's first breath,*
> *Cold and slow, endlessly timid, greedy*
> *For time but trembling, short-tempered, intolerant,*
> *Able to see only what they once saw, bitter*
> *To boys and men still growing old.*
> *Flowers bring fruit as they come,*
> *Take sweetness with them as they go.*
>
> *Epistles 2.3.153–178*

For the most part, the Greeks viewed old age with pessimism. The Romans viewed it with ambivalence, at best (Falkner and de Luce, 1992). We do find models of vigorous old age, however. Nestor in the *Iliad*, the oldest Greek at Troy, far from keeping silent in the presence of younger men, is not shy about offering his advice, and that advice is valued.

The most memorable positive image of masculine old age in Greek tradition may well be Cephalus in Plato's *Republic*. While Cephalus refers to the increased difficulty of getting around, he discounts other complaints about old age. Cephalus enjoys an old age of lively conversation and close associations with younger men; this is a peaceful life free from youthful passions. He concludes that his elderly friends' complaints about the barrenness of their lives should be attributed not to old age itself, but to individual character. But his comments apply only to men: Greek literature does not offer a comparable picture of old age for women.

For every Nestor or Cephalus, however, we find the more common depiction of old age as a time of loss, deprivation, and loneliness, as described, for example, by the chorus in Sophocles' *Oedipus at Colonus*:

> *And in the end he comes to strengthless age,*
> *Abhorred by all men, without company,*
> *Unfriended in that uttermost twilight*
> *Where he must live with every bitter thing.*
> *(1230–1238)*

The chorus is inspired by the painful old age of Oedipus—blind, in abject poverty, exiled, and dependent on his two young daughters. At the same time, Oedipus himself does not entirely match this vision of old age. Granted, he is frail and inspires fear, if not disgust, but he remains very much the man who answered the riddle of the Sphinx—opinionated, tough, determined, quick to anger. Moreover, as he walks unaided to his death, he transcends the chorus's gloomy assessment of old age.

Still, while we can hardly maintain that the old age of Oedipus was any more typical than his youth or middle age had been, this picture of an old man is not unique to this play. He reminds us of a recurring pattern that characterizes the vulnerablity and loss associated with old age—the pattern of elders mourning the deaths of their children. These elders share common features: They are often physically frail; they often experience considerable hardship, perhaps because they have lost a war, perhaps because they are in exile. We may wonder which is more significant in their lives, age or circumstances. Like Oedipus, they demonstrate moments of impressive courage and determination.

As the elderly mother of Euryalus mourns the death of her son in Virgil's *Aeneid*, she reminds us of the terrible loss for the family that the death of an adult child meant, as well as the plight of elders left without family members to care for them. Having followed him from Troy to Italy, she is now utterly alone:

> *You, evening peace of my last years, cruel son,*
> *how could you leave me here alone?...And I,*
> *your mother, did not follow*
> *you...*

> *(9.481–484)*

Laertes, in the *Odyssey*, lives in squalor, mourning his absent son. In book 24 of the *Iliad*, Priam musters the courage to enter the Greek camp alone and to claim from Achilles the body of Hector; the grieving father kisses the very hands of the man who killed his children. At the fall of Troy, Hecuba must endure the litany of deaths in her family, deaths that she witnesses—Hector, Priam, Polyxena, Astyanax. Though overwhelmed by grief and age, about to be taken slave to serve Penelope in Ithaca, Hecuba nonetheless exacts a horrible vengeance on Polymestor, the greedy friend who was responsible for the death and mutilation of her youngest son, left in his care.

Ovid's description of Hecuba reminds us of the grim fate she faces, but it also reminds us of the reservoirs of strength that these elders display. This is the same woman who wished that she could tear out with her teeth the liver of the man who had killed Hector. When she discovers the body of her youngest son, Hecuba rages with that same anger:

> *...as [the anger] flared,*
> *As though she still were queen, her sentence stood*
> *For vengeance, and the pictured punishment*
> *Filled all her thoughts...so Hecuba,*
> *Rage linked with grief, oblivious of her years*
> *But not her resolution, made her way to Polymestor...*
> *(Metamorphoses 13. 545–552)*

Comic tradition introduces other recurring images. Aristophanes ridicules indiscriminately the old men and women who make up the chorus in the Lysistrata. The old men are lecherous, querulous, constantly looking back with longing to the good old days of the Persian War, when they were young. On the other hand, the old women are an even match for the men; they are as tough, as determined, as vulgar. If anything, they are even more devious. Greed motivates Strepsiades, the old father in the *Clouds*, but he is too stupid to learn the lessons he needs to cheat his creditors, and his stupidity is equated with his age. Old men in Roman comedy frequently appear as acquisitive, devious, gullible, and lecherous and are frequently at odds with their sons (Falkner and de Luce, 1992).

Elders are ridiculed most frequently for their sexuality. In Aristophanes' *Congresswomen*, the old women concoct a scheme whereby handsome young men cannot pursue young women until they have slept with the old women. Cephalus may claim that it is a relief to be free of sexual appetite, but these old men and women are objects of ridicule precisely because they still have sexual appetites but have no opportunities to satisfy them. They violate the principle of *tempestivitas*: sexual pleasure is the province of the young.

Old women in Latin poetry are treated with a viciousness that far outstrips the portrayal of lustful old men, however. The normally genial Horace writes about an old woman with exuberant disgust:

> *Old bitch, stinking*
> *Old hag, asking me*
> *"How come you can't get it up?"*
> *You, with your black pit of a mouth,*
> *A forehead time plows with wrinkles,*
> *And a gaping ass, putrid between dried-up*
> *Haunches, gaping like a sick cow-hole!*
> *(Epode 8.1–6)*

Juvenal in *Satire 6* reviles old women who make love in Greek: In fact, the very possibility of their making love at all is unthinkable. Since women in Greece and Rome were valued primarily for their sexuality, while men were valued for their public accomplishments, it is no wonder that women's sexuality should assume such importance in these portraits of old age.

While we do not have sufficient evidence to confirm that the Greeks and Romans systematically discriminated against elders, we have enough evidence to suggest that elders enjoyed some privileges and respect by virtue of their age. At the same time, most people envisioned old age, rather as Virgil did, attended by grief, poverty, fear, and care. The persistence of this expectation may be most dramatically demonstrated in an unlikely source, Cicero's *On Old Age (Cato Maior de Senectute)*. This essay is arguably the oldest extant Western treatise on old age, but Cicero's readers would have recognized immediately the common ground it shares with the speech of Cephalus alone, just as the readers of Plutarch's essay on *Whether Old Men Should Participate in the State* would have recognized the influence of Cicero's essay. Cicero's spokesperson, 84-year-old Cato the Elder, confronts the four traditional complaints about old age: that it removes one from public life; brings the loss of physical strength; lacks pleasure, especially sensual pleasure; and is close to death. Like Cephalus, Cato distinguishes between the characteristics of old age and the characteristics of particular old men: Someone who was irascible, miserly, cautious in his youth will be irascible, miserly, and cautious in his old age. The best way to assure a comfortable, lively old age, he says, is to prepare for it in youth.

The elder's influence does not end with increasing frailty or retirement from official participation in public life. Cato describes an old age where the keenness of the intellect and experience in public life make the old man a desirable companion and advisor, particularly for younger men. Cicero's picture of old age cannot be taken as generic, however. This is an old age that only upper-middle-class, free, male citizens could have enjoyed. Not only does Cicero fail to mention any women in his essay (for reasons I cannot develop here), but it is highly unlikely that a woman would have been able to prepare for or enjoy such an old age (Hallett, 1991). In fact, Cicero himself did not enjoy an old age in keeping with Cato's description.

Cicero wrote his essay on old age when he was 62, on the heels of divorce from his second wife, and in enforced retirement from politics. What is even more important, Cicero wrote this, like many of his other philosophical works, while mourning the death of his daughter Tullia. In a very real sense he is like Priam, or Hecuba, or the mother of Euryalus. Mourning Tullia's death as much as the interruption of his participation in public life, he is painfully aware of his own age. As he tries to counter the arguments for why old age is an unhappy time, he reminds us even more forcefully of the prevailing negative attitude toward old age among the Greeks and Romans. We might ostensibly read this essay for encouragement as we prepare for our own old age, but the essay's real meaning lies in the fact that Cicero may be protesting entirely too much. Perhaps he realized that old age actually bore a striking resemblance to the negative traditional literary representations.

Where does this leave us? Whether or not we can label them as stereotypes, with all that that implies, we can find in Greco-Roman literary representations traditional images of old age. These vary according to genre, gender, and author's age, which are nowhere near as predictable as they appear at first glance, and include such varying characteristics as wisdom, great dignity in the face of irreparable loss, utter defeat, fear, desperate courage, physical weakness, rigidity, foolishness, sexual frustration. It remains to be seen whether these images informed actual policies that systematically discriminated against elders. If we are going to seek unambiguous roots of contemporary ageism, however, we should probably look someplace other than Greco-Roman antiquity.

References

Angel, J., 1972. "Ecology and Population in the Eastern Mediterranean" *World Archaeology* 4: 88–105.

Bertman, S., ed., 1976. *The Conflict of Generations in Ancient Greece and Rome.* Amsterdam: B. R. Gruner.

Bremmer, J., 1987. "The Old Women of Ancient Greece." In J. Blok and P. Mason, eds., *Sexual Asymmetry in Ancient Society.* Amsterdam: B. R. Gruner.

Butler, R. N., 1989. "Dispelling Ageism: The Cross-Cutting Intervention." *The Annals of the American Academy of Political and Social Science* 503:138–47.

de Luce, J., 1993, in press. "'Quod temptabam scribere versus erat': Ovid in Exile." In A. Wyatt-Brown and J. Rossen, eds., *Creativity, Aging and Gender in Literature of the Life Cycle.* Charlottesville: University of Virginia Press.

Falkner, T., and de Luce, J., eds., 1989. *Old Age in Greek and Latin Literature.* Albany: State University of New York Press.

Falkner, T., and de Luce, J., 1992. "A View From Antiquity: Greece, Rome, and Elders." In T. Cole et al., eds., *Handbook of Humanities and Aging.* New York: Springer Publishing Co.

Garland, R., 1990. *The Greek Way of Life: From Conception to Old Age.* Ithaca, N.Y.: Cornell University Press.

VARIETIES OF IMAGES AND PERCEPTIONS

Hallett, J., 1984. *Fathers and Daughters in Roman Society: Women and the Elite Family.* Princeton, N.J.: Princeton University Press.

Hallett, J., 1991. "Heeding Our Native Informants: The Use of Gender Literary Texts in Recovering Elite Roman Attitudes toward Age, Gender, and Social Status." Paper presented at Miami University, Oxford, Ohio.

Haynes, M. S., 1962. "The Supposedly Golden Age for the Aged in Ancient Greece (A Study of Literary Concepts of Old Age)." *Gerontologist* 2: 93–98.

Haynes, M. S., 1963. "The Supposedly Golden Age for the Aged in Ancient Greece (A Study of Literary Concepts of Old Age)." *Gerontologist* 3: 26–35.

Hopkins, K., 1966. "On the Probable Age Structure of the Roman Population." *Population Studies* 8: 245–64.

Kebric, R. B., 1983. "Aging Pliny's Letters: A View from the Second Century A.D." *Gerontologist* 23: 538–45.

Plescia, J., 1976. "*Patria Potestas* and the Roman Revolution." In I. S. Bertman, ed., *The Conflict of Generations in Ancient Greece and Rome.* Amsterdam: B. R. Gruner.

Schaps, D., 1979. *Economic Rights of Women in Ancient Greece.* Edinburgh: Edinburgh University Press.

Van Tassel, D., 1988. "Old Age, Leadership, and Gerontocratic Situations." *Case Western Reserve University Center on Aging and Health Newsletter* 10: 11–13.

Translations

Aristotle. *Poetics.* Translated by W. Hamilton Fyfe. Loeb Classical Library. Cambridge, Mass.: Harvard University Press, 1965 [1927].

The Essential Horace. Translated by B. Raffel. San Francisco: North Point Press, 1983.

Ovid. *Metamorphoses.* Translated by A. Melville. Oxford: Oxford University Press, 1986.

Sophocles. *Oedipus at Colonus.* Translated by R. Fitzgerald. In D. Grene and R. Lattimore, eds., *Sophocles I.* New York: Washington Square Press, 1973 [1954].

CHAPTER NINE

'And the Fear of the Poorhouse'

Perceptions of Old Age Impoverishment in Early Twentieth-Century America

Carole Haber

In 1934 the Committee on Economic Security, commissioned by President Franklin D. Roosevelt to examine the conditions of the aged in America, focused upon the growing number of elderly persons in the nation's almshouses. Displaying silhouette figures of older men with canes, the committee conclusively declared that the "predominance of the aged in almshouses is a sign of their increasing dependency" (Committee on Economic Security, 1934). The advanced years of a majority of inmates was then cited as dramatic proof of the need for an age-based pension system.

Pension advocates were not alone in relying upon the symbol of the almshouse to depict the supposedly increasing impoverishment of the old and their diminishing importance in industrializing society. In the late nineteenth century, a poem and a song, both entitled "Over the Hill to the Poorhouse," were published. One focused upon an elderly man, the other on an aged woman; both told the tales of upstanding elderly people who, deserted by children and too infirm to work, had little choice but to seek final refuge in the poorhouse (Carleton, 1871; Braham and Catlin, 1874). Filmmakers and photographers, as well, used the almshouse to underscore the precarious fate that awaited even the seemingly middle-class old (Griffith, 1911; Riis, 1890). Images of hollow-eyed old men and women sitting on threadbare cots filled the institutions' annual reports and weekly magazines; flowery prose detailed the horrible sights and smells confronting all who ventured inside. As a pervasive image, the almshouse evoked strong emotions. "The poorhouse," declared Abraham Epstein, an expert on aging, "stands as a threatening symbol of the deepest humiliation and degradation before all wage-earners after the prime of life" (Epstein, 1929, p. 128).

Great irony, however, lay beneath such popular images. Although nationally, as advocates for the old repeatedly stressed, the percentage of inmates *within* the asylum who were elderly grew dramatically from 33 percent in 1880 to 53 percent in 1904 and 67 percent in 1923, such statistics did not reveal that the old as a group were increasingly impoverished or displaced in modern society (Hoffman, 1909; Grob, 1986; Gratton, 1986). The percentage of all aged people in the United States who were institutionalized actually remained at about 2 percent; 98 percent of all old people continued to live beyond the institution's wall (Achenbaum, 1978; Haber, 1983). Yet the fact that most elderly people were not almshouse residents did not negate the important role the institution played in perceptions of the status of old age in America. The horror of the poorhouse cast a wide shadow. As this article will show, the very existence of the institution seemed to prove that a growing majority of elderly individuals faced poverty and dependence. As one government study noted in 1925, generations of Americans had grown up "with a reverence for God, the hope of heaven and the fear of the poorhouse" (Stewart, 1925, p. iii). Even for those who never set foot within the asylum, the threat of poorhouse residency had a power that could not be ignored and a potency that left a lasting impact on national perceptions and old age policies.

Although almshouses had been a part of the urban environment since the colonial era, they initially played a rather insignificant role in the welfare system. Municipal leaders placed the great majority of needy people with their kin or allotted them the necessary "outdoor" relief of a cord of wood, a supply of food, or a small monthly pension. Only the most destitute of the orphaned, insane, diseased, and elderly were sent to the poorhouse. Within the walls of the institution, however, little attempt was made to classify the inmates or reform their ways. In the eyes of the city fathers, these groups simply represented the most debilitated and hopeless of all the community's needy population (Rothman, 1971).

Beginning in the mid-nineteenth century, however, the almshouse took on increased importance. Beset by increasing numbers of impoverished immigrants, charity experts denounced the distribution of outdoor aid to the able-bodied and shiftless, as well as those in actual need. They broadly adopted the theory that alms pauperized the poor by making them lazy and dependent. As a result, civil leaders opposed all forms of outdoor relief and supported the building of forbidding almshouses and workhouses. Punitive institutions, they argued, would discourage the indolent and vicious from seeking charity and might "reform" those incarcerated under a strict code of conduct. Through their enforced discipline, they would warn the idle poor that hard work and a harsh regimen awaited all alms-seeking applicants (Clement, 1985).

Although the old were still assumed to be natural and rightful recipients of assistance, they fell victim to the authorities' antagonism against the idle young, foreign poor, and "vicious." Like other, although far less "deserving" individuals, they too were prohibited from receiving support in their own homes. With the establishment of the almshouse, welfare administrators gave them a choice: They could forgo applying for relief or agree to enter the purposefully punitive and noxious almshouse.

For those who entered the almshouse, mid-nineteenth-century welfare officials then attempted to enact the second component of institutional policy. Within asylums, and across institutions, they separated the inmates according to age, need, and character. Without proper separation of the needy, they argued, the vagrant would never be reformed into an industrious worker nor would the child be shaped into a self-sufficient adult (Katz, 1986).

To meet this goal, state and local authorities erected special institutions based on the perceived disabilities and handicaps of the inmates. Beginning with homes for the deaf, dumb, and blind in the 1830s, officials established a variety of institutions that removed large numbers of the dependent, although assumed reformable, individuals from the almshouse. Children were placed in orphanages or dispatched to the countryside, "juvenile delinquents" were assigned to reformatories, the acutely ill were transferred to hospitals, and "lunatics" were confined to asylums for the insane. In some cities, even able-bodied paupers were removed from the poorhouse and placed in workhouses designed to punish and reform. Here, city officials believed, they would find no more warm winters or free meals. Young and middle-aged adults would either learn to work or would suffer for their indolence (Rothman, 1971).

The establishment of harsh welfare policies and the creation of new institutions had a dramatic effect on the demographic composition of the almshouse. Without large numbers of children or young adults, the number of inmates within the asylum declined while the proportion of elderly inmates rose significantly. Immediately after the Civil War, for example, children made up 29 percent of inmates at the Charleston, South Carolina almshouse. In 1867, the great majority were removed to newly created orphanages. With the able-bodied already confined to a "Bettering House," and the insane placed in the state insane asylum, the poorhouse became filled primarily by the dependent old (City of Charleston, 1867; Haber and Gratton, 1987). Similarly, in late nineteenth-century San Francisco, the average age of the poorhouse residents rose from 37 in 1870 to 59 in 1894 (Smith, 1895).

By the early twentieth century, in fact, the transformation of the almshouse was well under way. In initially reorganizing the almshouse, welfare authorities had assumed that the greatest impact would be felt by the young and able-bodied, who would either decline relief or come under their control. Although, on an individual basis, almshouse relief was far more expensive than outdoor assistance, reformers imagined that their costs would be drastically cut; few, they assumed, would voluntarily choose the intentionally ominous almshouse. At the same time, welfare authorities removed individuals from the institution who, they believed, needed reform rather than punishment. In designing this system, officials hardly directed their wrath toward the old. Yet more than any other group, the debilitated elderly experienced the harsh consequences of the redesigned almshouse. Unlike the young, they were rarely judged to be capable of reform; unlike the able-bodied, they were hardly able to struggle on their own. Thus, as other individuals were placed in more attractive asylums—or attempted to remain outside the institution—the impoverished elderly became the institution's most prominent residents.

The transformation in the demographic composition of the almshouse was well noted and publicized. By the early twentieth century, local welfare authorities had come to recognize that their public institutions no longer housed diverse groups of inmates. In 1903, the Charity Board of New York City renamed its public almshouse the Home for the Aged and Infirm (Folks, 1903). In 1913, Charleston officials transformed their asylum into the "Charleston Home" (Charleston City Year Book, 1914, p. 311; Devine, 1909). The new names reflected a perception that went beyond the title on the door. In retitling the asylums, officials tied the institutions to the very nature of growing old in America. By 1925, the origins of almshouses as deterrents to the assumed laziness of the foreign-born and vicious had long been forgotten. The public institutions, a leading social analyst declared, were beginning to "fulfill the real purpose of an almshouse—that of providing [for] the old and infirm" (Stewart, 1925, p. 5).

The institutions became so linked with old age in America and their growing proportions of inmates so well publicized that numerous social scientists and welfare reformers began to study the institutions' population as a microcosm of poverty in America. Although they also charted national unemployment rates and levels of wealth, the almshouse served as the most tangible and heart-rending symbol of the elderly's plight. Through the wards of the almshouse, social scientists hoped to discover and publicize the impact of late nineteenth-century industrialization. Given the harsh conditions of the almshouse, they asked, and the worthy status of the old, why were the aged incarcerated at all?

In the search for answers, social analysts repeatedly made two critical and erroneous assumptions. First, seeing that the aged had become a majority of the American almshouse population, they assumed that poverty and dependency among the aged had also increased rapidly. In their charts and surveys of individuals *within* the institution, they emphasized the difficulties that awaited even the most providential aged worker. In contrast to past experts who had linked poverty to drink or laziness, they pronounced old age itself to be cause of dependency. Social reformers concluded that even those who struggled outside the asylum were, in time, likely to be institutionalized (Pennsylvania Commission on Old Age Pensions, 1919).

The first assumption of progressive analysts, however, appears to have had little real merit. The large number of elderly individuals in American almshouses was hardly proof that a sudden rise in poverty among the aged ever occurred. Nor did almshouse figures reveal that most elderly individuals would eventually come to depend on some form of public relief. Although the poorhouse population was increasingly composed of aged individuals, the proportion of the American aged who were incarcerated in them remained virtually unchanged between 1880 and 1920. As we have seen, the shift in the demographic composition of poorhouses was the result of specific bureaucratic and financial decisions made by politicians and welfare administrators, rather than rising dependency among the nation's aged population.

The first error, however, led to a second, and equally erroneous, supposition. Contemplating the assumed rising dependency among the old, and observing the coincident ascendancy of an industrial economy, progressive analysts charged that industrialization and urbanization were the sources of the elderly's new vulnerability. A host of critics asserted that as long as America had been a rural and agricultural land, the old had been greatly respected (Devine, 1898; Devine, 1904; Devine, 1909; Epstein, 1922; Epstein, 1929; Rubinow, 1913; Rubinow, 1934; Squier, 1912; Todd, 1915; Warner, 1894). The elderly's memory of the past was indispensable; their knowledge and skills had great value. In the modern world, however, the aged were left with few significant roles. Relegated to "the industrial scrapheap," the old were forced to end their lives confined in the nation's almshouses. In reality, however, this assumption was as inaccurate as the belief in the elderly's ever growing dependency. The economic transformation of the nation did not uniformly harm the elderly or deprive them of all resources (Haber and Gratton, in press).

Yet these errors did not limit the effectiveness of the reformers' arguments or the dominant role their assumptions played in calls for social reform. By the early twentieth century, inquiries into the causes of old age dependency began to produce consequences far beyond the limited number of inmates who were confined to the asylums' wards. Analysts argued that their investigations into almshouse conditions had important ramifications: long lists of individuals waiting to be placed in private institutions, worthy persons still forced to reside in almshouses, thousands of aged individuals who existed on the edge of poverty—all proved the increasing dependency of the elderly in the industrial world. Confusing the growing absolute numbers with unchanging proportions, analysts argued that almshouse residency had become a threat even to the hard-working middle class. In 1925, in her influential study *Aged Clients of Boston's Social Agencies*, Lucille Eaves asserted that "the risks of being left without means of meeting [the needs of] old age are not confined to the workers with low earning capacity but are shared by persons in all ranks of society" (Eaves, 1925, p. 3).

The power of such a belief was great indeed. In the early twentieth century, reformers used this pervasive view of old age poverty and the ominous almshouse as the basis for numerous reforms. They established old age homes to rescue worthy elderly individuals—usually of their own ethnic background—from the horrors of almshouse residency (Gratton, 1986; Haber, 1983). In addition, they tried to eliminate the perception that the almshouse was a punishment for the lazy and corrupt. By renaming the institution, and redecorating with flowers and plants, they tried to present the asylums as natural "homes" for the old (*Charleston City Year Book*, 1925).

Most important, reformers used the fear of the almshouse in the campaign for state annuities. In the pension movement, the almshouse became a symbol far larger than its inmate population. Advocates argued that the almshouse was both emotionally and financially corrupt. As an institution, it represented the callous treatment modern society awarded the elderly. As a deeply felt fear, it forced families to take extreme steps to avoid the incarceration of relatives. Pension advocates asserted that faced with a choice between allowing old relatives to enter the poorhouse or keeping necessary funds for themselves, adult children generally relinquished their own economic security and well-being. Family members even sacrificed the next generation by placing their own children in the labor market, at the expense of their future skills and education (Epstein, 1929; Lubove, 1968). Finally, advocates contended that the institution was fiscally irresponsible as it cost far less to support aged individuals in their own homes than in almshouses (U. S. Bureau of the Census, 1925; Stewart, 1925).

The provisions of the Social Security legislation clearly reflected these beliefs. Pension advocates had long argued that monthly payments would provide support for the old while finally eliminating the despised poorhouse. Even the Supreme Court relied upon these dual assertions when upholding the constitutionality of the Social Security Act. Writing for the majority in 1937, Justice Cardozo proclaimed that "the hope behind this statute is to save men and women from the rigors of the poorhouse as well as from the haunting fear that such a lot awaits them when journey's end is near" (*Helvering vs. Davis*, 1937).

Not surprisingly, then, restrictions written into the legislation ensured that almshouses could no longer exist (Snider, 1956). Social Security mandated that residents of public institutions were ineligible for any form of Old Age Assistance; all others, whether residing in private asylums, alone, or with families, could receive state and federal aid. Almost immediately states closed almshouses and returned aged persons to their families or placed them in private asylums or boarding houses—often with the same supervisors who had once overseen the operations of the poorhouses (Fischer, 1943). By 1950 the almshouse had finally been eliminated from the American welfare system.

The destruction of the almshouse marked a dramatic change in old age history. For over a century, the almshouse had loomed as a constant reminder of the heartless care society awarded the old. The increasingly elderly population of the almshouse seemed vivid proof of the growing impoverishment and neglect of the elderly. As a reality for some, and a symbol for many more, the institution had seemingly proved that the old were helpless victims of industrialization. While these beliefs were based on seriously flawed assumptions, they had a clear impact on public perceptions of the old. And, while the closing of the institution did not obliterate all fears of old age impoverishment, the destruction of the institution was significant. With the passage of the Social Security Act, the elderly no longer faced going "over the hill to the poorhouse"; the New Deal legislation finally shut the almshouse door.

References

Achenbaum, W. A., 1978. *Old Age in the New Land.* Baltimore, Md.: The Johns Hopkins Press.

Braham, D., and Catlin, G., 1874. "Over the Hill to the Poor House." In D. Scott and B. Wishy, eds., *America's Families: A Documentary History.* New York: Harper & Row, 1975.

Carleton, W., 1871. "Over the Hill to the Poorhouse." In G. Moss and W. Moss, eds., *Growing Old.* New York: Harper & Row, 1982.

Charleston City Year Book for 1913, 1914. Charleston, S.C.

Charleston City Year Book for 1924, 1925. Charleston, S.C.

City of Charleston, 1867. *Poor House Journal,* 15 May. Charleston, S.C.

Clement, P., 1985. *Welfare and the Poor in the Nineteenth-Century City.* Rutherford, N.J.: Fairleigh Dickinson University.

Committee on Economic Security, 1934. *The Need for Economic Security in the United States.* Washington, D.C.: Government Printing Office.

Devine, E. T., 1898. *Economics.* New York: Macmillan.

Devine, E. T., 1904. *The Principles of Relief.* New York: Macmillan.

Devine, E. T., 1909. *Misery and Its Causes.* New York: Macmillan.

Eaves, L., 1925. *Aged Clients of Boston's Social Agencies.* Boston: Women's Educational and Industrial Union.

Epstein, A., 1922. *Facing Old Age.* New York: Knopf.

Epstein, A., 1929. *The Problem of Old Age Pensions in Industry.* Harrisburg, Pa.: Pennsylvania Old Age Commission.

Fischer, V., 1943. "Kansas County Homes after the Social Security Act." *Social Service Review* 17: 442–65.

Folks, H., 1903. "Disease and Dependence." *Charities* 10: 499–500.

Gratton, B., 1986. *Urban Elders.* Philadelphia: Temple University Press.

Griffith, D. W., 1911. "What Shall We Do With Our Old." Movie available from the Metropolitan Museum of Art.

Grob, G., 1986. "Explaining Old Age History." In D. Van Tassel and P. N. Stearns, eds., *Old Age in a Bureaucratic Society.* Westport, Conn.: Greenwood Press.

Haber, C., 1983. *Beyond Sixty-Five.* New York: Cambridge University Press.

Haber, C., and Gratton, B., 1987. "Old Age, Public Welfare and Race." *Journal of Social History* 21: 263–79.

Haber, C., and Gratton B., in press. *Old Age and the Search for Security.* Bloomington, Ind.: Indiana University Press.

Helvering vs. Davis, 1937. W0 0-301, U.S. 619, Fall Term, United States Supreme Court.

Hoffman, F. L., 1909. "State Pensions and Annuities in Old Age." *Journal of the American Statistical Association* 11: 363–408.

Katz, M., 1986. *In the Shadow of the Poorhouse.* New York: Basic Books.

Lubove, R., 1968. *The Struggle for Social Security.* Cambridge, Mass.: Harvard University Press.

Massachusetts Commission on Pensions, 1925. *Report of Old-Age Pensions.* Boston: Commonwealth of Massachusetts.

Pennsylvania Commission on Old Age Pensions, 1919. *Report.* Harrisburg, Pa.: Kuhn Publishing.

Riis, J., 1890. *How the Other Half Lives.* New York: Scribner's.

Rothman, D., 1971. *The Discovery of the Asylum.* Boston: Little, Brown.

VARIETIES OF IMAGES AND PERCEPTIONS

Rubinow, I. M., 1913. *Social Insurance.* New York: Holt.

Rubinow, I. M., 1930. "The Modern Problem of the Care of the Aged." *Social Service Review* 4: 178.

Rubinow, I. M., 1934. *The Quest for Security.* New York: Holt.

Smith, M. R., 1895. "Almshouse Women." *American Statistical Association* 4: 219–62.

Snider, C. F., 1956. "The Fading Almshouse." *National Municipal Review:* 60–65.

Squier, L. W., 1912. *Old Age Dependency in the United States.* New York: Macmillan.

Stewart, E. M., 1925. *The Cost of American Almshouses.* Washington, D.C.: U. S. Bureau of Labor Statistics, Bulletin No. 386.

Todd, A. J., 1915. "Old Age and the Industrial Scrap Heap." *American Statistical Association* 14:550–57.

U. S. Bureau of the Census, 1925. *Paupers in the Almshouse: 1923.* Washington, D.C.: Government Printing Office.

Warner, A., 1894. "The Causes of Poverty Further Considered." *American Statistical Association* 4: 49–68.

Images of Aging

A Cross-Cultural Perspective

Jay Sokolovsky

Even a cursory look at global and historical data on the aging process provides testimony to the great variety and complexity of the ways in which images of aging are formed and reflected in the realities of an elder citizen's life. While for classical Greek culture, aging was deemed an unmitigated misfortune, among the Samoans being a healthy old person was the pinnacle of life (Holmes and Rhoads, 1987). Whereas the Greeks not only said, "Whom the gods love, die young," and invented various myths to support this notion (Slater, 1964), Samoan adults could not fully enter many of the most important realms of their culture until the fifth and sixth decades of life.

As revealed by the cross-cultural examination of imagery connected to aging, the non-Western vision of the aging process and old people not only indicates the divergence from our own perceptions of aging but points to critical intrasocietal distinctions based on gender and perceived phases of late adulthood. It is becoming clear that culturally constructed perceptions of becoming old, being old, and fading into a stage of nonfunctioning senescence can have dramatic implications for how a given society metaphorically thinks about its elders. In exploring these issues, I will first examine how cultural variation relates to created images of aging and the aged and then consider how images of the culturally nonfunctional aged interact with societal reaction to such persons.

CULTURE, IMAGE, CONTEXT, AND AGING

A growing body of research highlights the importance of understanding the nature of the aging experience within an appropriate cultural context. There is no simple association between preindustrial/premodern societies and a particular image of aging. Each cultural system acts as a set of symbolic constructs through which a particular version of reality is perceived. In this way any sociocultural system establishes the collective representations and values that shape, and in turn are shaped by, distinct patterns of political economy, kinship, and ritual behavior. Also at work are contextual factors that can alter how cultures transform people's lives. Therefore, one must always be cognizant of how such variables as degree of family support, gender, or class position might alter the images associated with aging in a single society.

The basis for culturally constructing images of aging stems from the dependence of human communities on high levels of prolonged material and social interdependence among generations. This connection of people in different parts of the life cycle is universally recognized by age-linked language categories, such as child, adult, and old person. The variable definitions of when and how persons move through such markers of age-based status strongly shape the culturally differentiated perceptions of time, aging, and generation and are vitally linked to the cherished myths each culture possesses (Fry and Keith, 1982; Kertzer, 1982; Foner, 1984; Kertzer and Schaie, 1989: Fry, 1990).

Social boundaries associated with age-based statuses show great variation in the degree to which they allot power and create images invoking separation among the differently named categories of persons. For example, the Mbuti pygmy hunter-gatherers of Zaire have four loosely defined age grades (categories): children, youths, adults, and older persons (Turnbull, 1965). No elaborate rituals mark the passage from one grade to another, and no barriers prevent easy interaction between those in different age categories. Still, well-known norms do shape the behavior and responsibility assumed to be the preserve of a given grade. The Mbuti have created a potent, positive, but nonhierarchical image of the aged, who as a category of person are called mangese—"the great ones." Their culture contains one of the most balanced, egalitarian systems for linking generations that is known in the ethnographic literature.

In contrast, one can find societies where age grades are transformed into sharply ascribed age sets. Here different spans along the life cycle are sharply set apart by highly managed images involving spectacular ritual, distinct dress, and specialized tasks, modes of speech, comportment, and deferential gestures. Persons move through the life cycle collectively and form tightly bound groups performing specific tasks. The most elaborated forms of such cultural systems are found among East African nomadic herders, such as the Samburu of Kenya (Spencer, 1965). Here age sets of males initiated together move through the life cycle collectively. Over time and through elaborate ritual, they progressively take on, as a group, age-bounded roles of herders, warriors, and various grades of elders. Male elders in their fifth and sixth decades gain substantial power through maintaining large polygynous households, holding wealth in their numerous cattle, and having a ritual link to the ancestors, whom they can call upon to supernaturally curse younger persons who misbehave. As is the case for most such age-based societies, Samburu women's social maturation is accomplished through individual life cycle rituals, and their status is much more tied to their place in family units (see Kertzer and Madison, 1981, for the rarer case of women's age sets).

All too often, such cultures have been held up as exemplars of places where a strong positive image of the elderly reaches its zenith. It is important to note that this is frequently accomplished at the expense of intense intergenerational conflict, exploiting and repressing the young, and preventing women from gaining an equitable place in the community. Among the Samburu, older women in fact do not share the very powerful image associated with old men. When they are widowed, women are not permitted to marry again and suffer both materially and socially. Elder widows are more apt to be characterized as "old donkeys" rather than as paragons of moral strength and virtue (Fratkin, 1983, personal communication).

THE IMAGE OF OLD

The conception of being "old" is almost universal and is culturally constructed by a variety of measures. Only one study to date has systematically used worldwide data, contained in the Human Relations Area Files, to examine this issue. In this study, anthropologists Anthony Glascock and Susan Feinman (1981) found that in a random sample of 60 societies there were three basic means of identifying a category of "old":

change of social/economic role, chronology, and change in physical characteristics. Particularly striking in this work are the following conclusions:

1. A change in social/economic role is by far the most common marker of becoming old. This can include one's children becoming parents, general shifts in the types of productive activities one engages in, or beginning to receive more goods and services than one produces.

2. A change in capabilities is the least common marker. Factors such as invalid status and senility are quite rare as primary indicators of a general designation of old. This seems to be the case because societies frequently create a category of old that begins before many people encounter such radical signs of physical decline.

3. Almost a majority of societies in the sample have multiple definitions of being aged. These varied definitions of aging are commonly applied to distinct categories of "old," which include a phase of aging linked to movement toward the loss of normal functioning and death.

This last item seems to add a component of both complexity and ambiguity to how societies fully flesh out their images of aging. As we will see later on, confronting an image of the old tilted to the dimensions of incapacity and death can initiate drastic changes in the attitudes and behavior exhibited toward those so labeled.

Mythic Images of the Elderly

In preindustrial societies, where people existed without situation comedies or Pepsi commercials, orally conveyed folktales often transmitted complex symbolic messages about different parts of the life cycle. Not infrequently, the mythic images of the elderly were of sacred personages who inhabit a close-by nether world and who watch over human endeavors. For example, the hunting/gathering Inuit of arctic North America not only tended to glorify elders in folktales, but the majority of gods, heroes, and demons depicted were prototypically ancient adults. The polar Eskimo, for example, believed an old woman named Nerivik to be a goddess who lives beneath the water. She would thwart the efforts of the young seal hunters until the village shaman made a cosmic voyage to visit her and comb her matted hair. Only then could the seals swim through her sacred hairdo and be caught (Holmes 1983, p. 89). Another myth of a related Inuit people tells of an old man who was transfigured into a luminous body and shot up into the sky, where he then existed as a bright guiding star to hunters.

Of course, such mythic images of aged figures must be balanced against the overall Inuit cultural context in which it is actually the virile, young adult male hunter who is the object of social cynosure and against whom ultimate prestige is measured (Guemple, 1987).

In his study of the Qigiktamuit Inuit of Labrador, Guemple found that while the aged in general were viewed as resources for extra labor, repositories of valuable knowledge, and means of social control, the transition, especially for males, to being regarded as old (*ituk*) took place early (late 40s to early 50s) and was resisted with a variety of "renewal" activities. This package of "image management" ranged from ostentatious generosity with hunted game to the taking of a young wife. Adult females tended not to be called old woman (*niñgui*) until they were past age 55–60 and seemed to have a longer transition to being so labeled. Not so burdened with the comparison to the ideal male model, older females appeared less apt to pursue renewal activities; if they did, these most typically involved the adoption of children. While many older women were seen as having garnered special esoteric powers, especially for curing, when things went wrong in a village it was such aged females who were most likely to be blamed for misfortune.

It is noteworthy that in societies such as the Mbuti or pre-1960s Japan, where the general image of the aged was about as positive as one finds in the range of human societies, myths and folktales existed that projected dire consequences for straying from age norms. In the Mbuti case there is a tale of a misfit elder who is buried alive. Among the Japanese there is the story of Old Rin, made famous by the Japanese novel, *The Oak Mountain Song*. In the folktale, people in this poor isolated rural area are required at age 70 to go to Oak Mountain to await death. Old Rin is only 69 and very healthy, but her son thinks she is a burden and urges her to make the suicidal pilgrimage. To look the part of the very old, Rin knocks out some teeth and trudges up the mountain to die. Interestingly, this tale has various endings: (1) the son suffers remorse and rescues Rin; (2) the son arrives too late and finds Rin dead; and (3) the son hides Rin and uses her knowledge to solve a problem of the king, who then grants his wish to end abandonment of the elderly (Plath, 1972).

THE FEMININE TRIAXIAL MYSTIQUE

One of the critical issues to consider in a cross-cultural look at images of aging is the divergent metaphors created on the basis of gender.

VARIETIES OF IMAGES AND PERCEPTIONS

Predominant in many societies is the hydra-headed perception of older women. Within one society, they may be viewed in a variety of seemingly contradictory ways, with images that range from the positive, nurturing matriarch/granny to a mystical shamaness and finally to the feared evil witch. Such variant depictions of female elderhood seem most glaring in patrilineal societies, especially those that fuse a public image for older males to the cultural heights of prestige and respect. A number of authors have commented on patterns of gender role reversal that originate when women enter their postreproductive phase and culminate when mastery of the domestic sphere is complete. This is typically marked by control of the daughter-in-law and other adult female kin. It is further enhanced by influence over married sons and their children, greater authority over rituals regulating social ties (especially life cycle events), and the gradual movement of a woman's spouse out of his public domain and into her hearth-centered life (Kerns and Brown, 1992; Cool and McCabe, 1987; Gutmann, 1987). This can be coupled with selective forays into public arenas, previously off limits to these women as premenopausal females. As Silverman notes, "even in male-dominated societies, like the Comanche in North America, the Mundurucu of South America and the Ewe of West Africa, women who have reached menopause fill important decision-roles otherwise restricted to men" (Silverman, 1987, p. 335). A classic description of this process is provided by Kaberry (1939) in an early anthropological study of Australian aboriginal women. Here she observed how as women become senior adults, they often assume greater authority within and outside their own extended kin network. They were observed functioning as arbiters of tribal law and taking the initiative in establishing order when community disputes raged out of control.

A dramatic alternation between images projecting a "Dear Old Thing" versus the "Scheming Hag" now abounds in the ethnographic literature (Cool and McCabe, 1987). Public metaphors depicting aging women seem to be more divergent and dramatic than the cultural images created for men. This is likely related to the preponderance of male-dominated societies and the consequent greater ability of males to manipulate public images. A graphic example of this was the disproportionate projection of an image of "witch" on middle-aged and older women during the Middle Ages (Bever, 1982).

THE 'NEAR DEAD'—
IMAGE MANAGEMENT'S ULTIMATE CHALLENGE

Leo Simmons, in his opus on global patterns of aging, states the following:

Among all peoples a point is reached in aging at which any further use-fulness appears to be over, and the incumbent is regarded as a living lia-bility. "Senility" may be a suitable label for this. Other terms among prim-itive peoples are the "over aged," the "useless stage," the "sleeping peri-od," "the age grade of the dying," and the "already dead" (1960, p. 87).

Worldwide comparative studies have corroborated the commonality of such distinctions (Maxwell and Maxwell, 1980; Maxwell, Silverman and Maxwell, 1982; Glascock, 1990). This research has also demonstrated a potent connection between such altered images of aging and dramatically changed attitudes toward individuals. Even societies that give high praise for the general concept of aging and provide valued roles for the active, healthy elderly may not only quickly withdraw cultural forms of esteem for the "over aged" but even direct forms of contempt and "death-hastening" measures toward such elderly. In a crucial comparative study of the reasons for showing contempt toward the elderly, Maxwell and Maxwell (1980) iso-lated eight types of complaints leveled against the aged as rationales for the display of negative treatment. While physical deterioration was a significant variable in explaining the variance in expressed contempt, it lagged behind "loss of family support system" and "devalued appearance" in accounting for the vagaries of negative behavior shown the elderly. The authors suggest that a negatively altered physical image of the old may be a far more impor-tant factor than has been expected in understanding the construction and deconstruction of personhood in late life (Barker, 1990).

CONCLUSIONS

This chapter has suggested how culture and context can serve to trans-form the societally construed image of the aged. It has shown that consid-eration of certain variables is critical in any analysis of how the elderly are portrayed. These crucial variables have to do with the ways in which cul-tures (1) create social boundaries between generations, (2) distribute power between the genders over the life cycle, and (3) use mythology. Finally, this chapter has suggested that one of the most difficult dilemmas any society must deal with is how to manage the image of the frail, very old individual. Image management of this category of person has perhaps the most potential for producing harm to those least able to cope with psychological threats to their personhood.

References

Barker, J., 1990. "Between Humans and Ghosts: The Decrepit Elderly in a Polynesian Society." In J. Sokolovsky, ed., *The Cultural Context of Old Age: World-Wide Perspectives*. New York: Bergin and Garvey.

Bever, E., 1982. "Old Age and Witchcraft in Early Modern Europe." In P. Sterns, ed., *Old Age in Preindustrial Society*. New York: Holmes and Meier.

Cool, L., and McCabe, J., 1987. "The 'Scheming Hag' and the 'Dear Old Thing': The Anthropology of Aging Women." In J. Sokolovsky, ed., *Growing Old in Different Societies*. Acton, Mass.: Copley.

Foner, N., 1984. *Ages in Conflict: A Cross-Cultural Perspective on Inequality Between Old and Young*. New York: Columbia University Press.

Fry, C., 1990. "The Life Course in Context: Implications of Research." In R. Rubinstein, ed., *Anthropology and Aging: Comprehensive Reviews*. Dordrecht, Netherlands: Kluwer.

Fry, C., and Keith, J., 1982. "The Life Course as a Cultural Unit." In M. Riley, ed., *Aging from Birth to Death: Interdisciplinary Perspectives*, vol. 2. Boulder, Colo.: Westview Press.

Glascock, A., 1990. "By Any Other Name It Is Still Killing: A Comparison of the Treatment of the Elderly in America and Other Societies." In J. Sokolovsky, ed., *The Cultural Context of Old Age: World-Wide Perspectives*. New York: Bergin and Garvey.

Glascock, A., and Feinman, S., 1981. "Social Asset or Social Burden: An Analysis of the Treatment of the Aged in Non-Industrial Societies." In C. Fry, ed., *Dimensions: Aging, Culture and Health*. New York: Praeger.

Guemple, D., 1987. "Growing Old in Inuit Society." In J. Sokolovsky, ed., *Growing Old in Different Societies*. Acton, Mass.: Copley.

Gutmann, D., 1987. *Reclaimed Powers: Toward a New Psychology of Men and Women in Later Life*. New York: Basic Books.

Holmes, L., 1983. *Other Cultures' Elder Years: An Introduction to Cultural Gerontology*. Minneapolis, Minn.: Burgess.

Holmes, L., and Rhoads, E., 1987. "Aging and Change in Samoa." In J.

Sokolovsky, ed., *Growing Old in Different Societies*. Acton, Mass.: Copley.

Kayberry, P., 1939. *Aboriginal Women: Sacred and Profane*. London:Rutledge and Sons.

Kerns, V., and Brown, J., 1992. *In Her Prime: New Views of Middle-Aged Women*. Urbana, Ill.: University of Illinois Press.

Kertzer, D., 1982. "Generation and Age in Cross-Cultural Perspective." In M. Riley, ed., *Aging From Birth to Death*, vol. 2. Boulder, Colo.: Westview Press.

Kertzer, D., and Madison, O. B. B., 1981. "Women's Age-Set Systems in Africa:The Latuka of Southern Sudan." In C. Fry, ed., *Dimensions: Aging, Culture and Health*. Brooklyn, N.Y.: Praeger.

Kertzer, D., and Schaie, K. W., 1989. *Age Structuring in Comparative Perspective*. Hillsdale, N.J.: Lawrence Erlbaum.

Maxwell, E., and Maxwell, R., 1980. "Contempt for the Elderly: A Cross-Cultural Analysis." *Current Anthropology* 24: 569–70.

Maxwell, R., Silverman, P. and Maxwell, E., 1982. "The Motive for Gerontocide." In J. Sokolovsky, ed., *Aging and the Aged in the Third World: Part I Studies in Third World Societies*, No. 22. Williamsburg, Va.: College of William and Mary.

Plath, D., 1972. "Japan: The After Years." In D. Cowgill and L. Holmes, eds., *Aging and Modernization*. New York: Appleton-Century-Crofts.

Silverman, P., ed., 1987. *The Elderly as Modern Pioneers*. Bloomington and Indianapolis, Ind.: Indiana University Press.

Simmons, L., 1945. *The Role of the Aged in Primitive Society*. New Haven, Conn.: Yale University Press.

Simmons, L., 1960. "Aging in Primitive Societies: A Comparative Survey of Family Life and Relationships." In C. Tibbetts, ed., *Handbook of Social Gerontology: Societal Aspects of Aging*. Chicago, Ill.: University of Chicago Press.

Slater, P., 1964. "Cross-Cultural Views of the Aged." In R. Kastenbaum, ed., *New Thoughts on Old Age*. New York: Springer Publishing Co..

Spencer, P., 1965. The Samburu: *A Study of Gerontocracy in a Nomadic Tribe*. Berkeley, Calif.: University of California Press.

Turnbull, C., 1965. *Wayward Servants*. New York: Natural History Press.

CHAPTER ELEVEN

The Last Quilting Bee

Iris Carlton-LaNey

About 13 years ago, the women who lived in Crosspoint (pseudonym for a small farming community in southeastern North Carolina) had their last quilting bee. It did not require long planning or preparation. The hostess, my mother, simply made a few telephone calls to her sister/friends, asking them to come over to help her "put in a quilt." Mama had made the top of the quilt by sewing together scraps of fabric that she had acquired over time. Making quilt tops was a solitary activity, which Mama had completed before calling on her friends. There was no elaborate design; she simply wanted to be able to give a quilt to each of her daughters.

The room was prepared for her guests with the quilt stretched out, attached to a wooden frame pulled tightly and propped up on chairs stationed at each of the four corners. All the chairs from the kitchen and dining room were brought into the family room where the quilt waited. Aunt Eva, Cousin Bertha, Cousin Lucy Mae, and Miss Jewel all arrived about the same time. After greeting them, Mama apologized for the quilt's not being fancy—"just something for the children." As they all took their seats around the quilting frame, Mama offered them coffee and cake. The one can of beer in the refrigerator had been saved for Miss Jewel. "She enjoys a beer," the women remarked to each other.

The quilting went on for hours with little discussion of it save a few comments about Aunt Eva's not being able to see too well and her own complaints that her "lines weren't straight." There were also comments about aching joints, weakness in the hands, and a concern that the thread wouldn't be tight enough. Together, they would periodically roll the frame inward as the quilting progressed closer to the center and would ask Mama for additional thread. Each woman had brought her own quilting needle.

The conversation brought the room to life with voices of elderly women laughing and joking but carefully listening as they worked together toward the completion of a common goal. I had no role except to wait on them, to listen, and to observe the beauty of the occasion, which I believed they felt would be their last quilting party together. They talked on for hours about their lives, joys, children, and church, with talk of their husbands as the dominant theme. They complained, reminisced, and laughed about their menfolk. Now and then, they'd slip in a little "sex talk," then, overcome with embarrassment laced with snickers, they'd look over at me and comment that they needed to shut their mouths, "with that young'un sitting over there." The "young'un" was nearly 30 years old.

I have thought a lot more about that event during the past 13 years—not just as a daughter, niece, or cousin but as a researcher. I have come to realize the deeper meaning and implications of that quilting bee and their other activities together as neighbors, friends, child brides, relatives by marriage, and sisters through common shared experience. Their talk over the work of quilting was of as much importance as the quilt itself. During their conversations, "they shared small truths," the way that women do mainly with other women. They also actively listened to each other, reserving judgment and often leaving the "weighty" in the "hands of the Lord." Their talk was neither lofty nor intellectual. Rather, it was conversation among and between intimates. It was "real talk," the kind that reached deep into the heart, soul, and experiences of each other. It was the kind of talk that drew out the explorations, analyses, and caring from each; and each participated. They did not solve the problems of the world, nor was that their intent; rather, they reinforced healing ties among sisters.

In the 13 years since that quilting bee, the quality of life of many of these women has deteriorated, and age has brought many changes. Some have moved out of the small farming community because of illness or death of a spouse. One of the women recently died. But their love and caring for one another remain. They telephone each other occasionally. But the telephone was never the first choice for contact and was never perceived as a mechanism for visiting friends. Rather, it actually represented a barrier to the desired personal contact and hands-on experience that provided the positive reaffirmation of self these women desired. For them, "real talk" took place face-to-face. It was the Sunday afternoon visits that nurtured and helped to sustain them. They often speak of how much they miss each other and of how much meaning each has given to the others' lives. Because of health problems like anxiety disorders, vision impairment, and arthritis, they are less mobile and the Sunday afternoon visits have ceased, along with the quilting bees. These women have managed hard lives with help from understanding sisters; but now social isolation and loneliness are issues they must confront.

Their quilts have been passed from mother to daughter. As we, the daughters, look at or use each quilt, we are reminded and feel the spirit of the quilting bee. That spirit represents a sense of oneness, collective identity and sisterhood for African-American women, regardless of age.

As a researcher, I continue my efforts to discover and understand the "social truths" about aging women, particularly aging African-American women in the rural south. Gould (1989) recommends a minority-feminist perspective as a guide to better understanding and planning for this group of aging women. This perspective involves the development of a culturally sensitive model that examines cultural differences and minority group stature jointly but "within" the context of a female experience.

The prevailing perceptions of the African-American elderly must also be examined for a better understanding of this population. Current themes in gerontological literature suggest that elderly African-Americans develop and use an array of coping mechanisms as well as personal and systemic resources. Essentially, elderly African-Americans are perceived as effective copers and survivors (Gibson, 1986; Chatters and Taylor, 1989) who function within supportive extended family networks (Barresi and Menon, 1991; Johnson, Gibson and Luckey, 1990). Because of the mutual aid system inherent in the extended family, it is also believed that elderly African-Americans in rural areas do not use formal helping services extensively (Goodfellow, 1983; Carlton-LaNey, 1991). Furthermore, religion and religious behavior are said to constitute a significant part of this population's life and coping ability (Taylor, 1986; Gibson, 1986; Haber, 1984).

Analyzing an activity like the quilting bee can help to provide some additional understanding of this group, their perceptions of work, and their perceptions of their own aging. It is significant to add that this author has had a lifelong, intimate relationship with these women. Because of my relationship with them, they were completely at ease during the research process. This essay is, therefore, based on the quilting bee as well as the author's observations of and involvement with this group of southern women over many years (Carlton-LaNey, 1989).

Several important themes about work, interpersonal relationships, and growing old surfaced from this observation and from my knowledge of this group. First, there exists a strong work orientation and commitment to work for family income and for family sustenance. Second, these farm women experience themselves in terms of relationships and connections to others. Finally, aging is viewed as a period of transition where multiple losses are coped with through prayer.

PERCEPTIONS OF WORK

From observing the quilting bee, one could tell that these women have always approached life in very practical and resourceful ways. Quilting was simply another form of women's work. As Miller (1984) notes, each quilt is an individual creation, although neighbors may share scraps of fabric and patterns. For most of the women of Crosspoint, quilting was done primarily to provide bedcovers for warmth during winter; essentially, it involved the production of utilitarian quilts. If the colors were bright and the patterns fancy, then perhaps the process was enhanced; but these were never prerequisites. In addition to quilting as part of rural women's work, it was also a way for these women to socialize with each other. It gave the women an opportunity to visit with each other while engaging in useful and productive work. One of the quilting women made this statement when asked about her work as a farm woman.

> In the wintertime, we'd sew quilt scraps for our work. Then it would come kinda a warm day, we'd put in a quilt and we'd quilt that out. Had to buy batts of cotton...put it between the top and the lining and sit down with a needle and thread and sew it all the way across, making circles. We'd help each other make quilts. We made ourselves useful through the years from one thing to the other. Neighbors worked together. If it hadn't been for the neighbors working together, I don't see how we would have made it.

These women perceived of work as a communal activity. While they had many hours of solitary work, their eyes light up when they talk of farmwork with neighbors and friends. Statements reflecting regrets were infrequent. Instead, they often expressed great pride in their ability to do farm tasks well and quickly.

Harvesting tobacco was the major and most labor-intensive farm task for these women. Tobacco was the primary cash crop. Women and children typically worked at the tobacco barn "looping" the tobacco onto sticks with twine. Talk around the tobacco trucks was usually lively and enjoyable. Women often used that time to socialize younger women to acceptable and appropriate behavior, to transmit values, and to comfort and reassure each other. With regard to this specific task, one woman stated, "Some parts of [farm] work we enjoyed because we worked with each other. When we'd be putting in tobacco, we enjoyed it because we'd always be with community people."

PERCEPTIONS OF RELATIONSHIPS

The quilting bee is an excellent illustration of peer relationships centered around a group activity. Activity theory supports the premise that activities provide the role support that is needed for the maintenance of a positive self-concept, which is correlated with high morale. Sterne and colleagues (1974) provided data suggesting, however, that friendships of African-American elderly may not involve the interpersonal intimacy and the resulting role supports needed to sustain morale. Creecy and Wright (1979) concluded similarly that informal activity with friends was not associated with morale among elderly African Americans. The findings of research investigating the relationship between friendships and morale are mixed. The likelihood that, among rural elderly African Americans, the term "friend" is used loosely may help to account for the inconsistency of these findings. This assumption is supported by several research studies (Sterne, Phillips and Raushka, 1974; Creecy and Wright, 1979). On the other hand, interaction at the Crosspoint quilting bee, along with prior and subsequent observations, suggests that intimate friendships and morale are closely related. Blau (1981) supports this finding, noting that peer relationships rather than filial relationships determine morale in old age. The group of women of Crosspoint form a friendship group that functions as a social support network of natural helpers. Preston and Mansfield (1984) observed that closeness among individuals in a social network serves to promote feelings of security that help reduce stress. The Crosspoint quilting bee is one example of ways that these women took care of each other's emotional needs. It helped them to avoid social isolation and provided a time to "lighten one's personal burden" through

99

interactions and conversations with equals. It was a time for "visiting," "catching up," and strengthening healing ties among kin.

In addition to the quilting bees, the women also gathered for their monthly meetings of the Crosspoint Home Demonstration Club. (The State Council of Home Demonstration Clubs of North Carolina, organized in 1940 and renamed the North Carolina Extension Homemakers Association in 1974, is a voluntary statewide community-based organization that is solidly integrated into the social fabric of rural America. The Crosspoint Club, now defunct, was part of this larger state organization.) Through the club these women learned new and different ways to care for their homes and families. The club, a much more formal group than the quilting bee, also gave them opportunities to socialize.

A county agent usually met with the group, facilitated the meetings, and demonstrated specific activities such as appropriate canning or sewing techniques. The meetings rotated to each member's home, and the hostess prepared a special lunch for her guests. While the women enjoyed the group learning activities, some reminisced that the meetings were one of the "few times that the women had to get together" outside of work-related gatherings. In addition to the educational component, the women of Crosspoint remembered the "eating together" and their talks during the meals as the most fun. They appreciated the input from the agent, but quickly added that they "really enjoyed themselves" when she was not present because they felt less inhibited and could enjoy each other without intrusion from an outsider. The women no longer meet as a club for the same health reasons that ended the quilting bees. Essentially, each opportunity that the women of this community had to get together strengthened their relationships and enhanced their social support network of natural helpers. These women formed a strong, natural bond of fictive kin that occurred because of proximity, necessity, and sameness.

PERCEPTIONS OF AGING

The women of Crosspoint view aging as a natural and "blessed" time in their lives. It is simply a transitional period for them. As Gibson (1986) noted, aging among older African-Americans is not a crisis; it is facilitated by a "well-oiled machinery" of helpers that includes a multiple use of family members and other substitute helpers. Similarly, Taylor and Chatters (1986) indicated that Southern older African-Americans have larger informal helper networks than their counterparts in other regions of the country. That network includes both family and friends.

The women of Crosspoint usually speak of aging within the context of God, family, and support network. Their comments include the following:

"I thank God I can still wait on myself and my husband."

"I can say I've had a good life 'cause my daughters try to help take care of me. If it wasn't for my daughters, I don't know what I would do."

"We had it tough, but we made it somehow...the Lord has spared us to come this far. I can say we were blessed by the merciful God."

The "well-oiled machinery" to which Gibson (1986) refers exists for the women of Crosspoint and helps to ease their transition into old age. Their mutual aid system remains intact although some of the players are different. One Crosspoint resident recalls that her son "comes out here to see about us just about every day." Another woman who has moved out of the small farming community into a nearby town with her daughter and family smiles with pride and a sense of security when she states that she does not participate in the congregate meals program only a fraction of a mile from her home, because her son-in-law "dared" her to go, saying that he could feed her when she got hungry.

CONCLUSION

In sum, the women of Crosspoint rely on a combination of prayer and a social support network of natural helpers to make the transition into old age. The quilting bee is an illustration of this complex support system of rural elderly African-American women. Understanding such an activity can provide information useful for policy development and program planning. The quilting bee suggests, for example, that this group of women enjoy communal work and useful work. Activities perceived of as useless and solitary may get little participation. Furthermore, this friendship group of women has tended to provide empathy and a sense of connectedness for each woman. Their comments around issues of aging and health not only reflect these feelings of connectedness and interdependence, but in ways make formal helping systems seem unnecessary and unacceptable. Such perceptions may account for the paucity of services tailored to meet this group's needs. These women have learned to rely on each other for help, advice, and services. Interventions from outside must, therefore, be sensitive to being perceived as intrusive. Moreover, such interventions must be culturally sensitive and female-centered, with a carefully planned outreach component that involves familiar and valued resources like church and family.

References

Barresi, C., and Menon, G., 1991. "Diversity in Black Family Caregiving." In Z. Harel, E. McKinney and M. Williams, eds., *Black Aged.* Newberry Park, Calif.: Sage.

Blau, Z., 1981. *Old Age in a Changing Society.* New York: Franklin Watts.

Carlton-LaNey, I., 1989. *Elderly Black Farm Women as Keepers of the Community and the Culture.* Greensboro, N.C.: Appletex Educational Center.

Carlton-LaNey, I., 1991. "Some Considerations of the Rural Elderly Black's Underuse of Social Services." *Journal of Gerontological Social Work* 16(1/2): 3–17.

Chatters, L., and Taylor, R., 1989. "Life Problems and Coping Strategies of Older Black Adults." *Social Work* 34(4): 313–19.

Creecy, R., and Wright, R., 1979. "Morale and Informal Activity with Friends Among Black and White Elderly." *Gerontologist* 19(6): 544–47.

Gibson, R., 1986. "Older Black Americans." *Generations* 10(4): 35–39.

Goodfellow, M., 1983. "Reasons for Use and Nonuse of Social Services Among the Rural Elderly." *Human Services in the Rural Environment* 8(4): 10–16.

Gould, K., 1989. "A Minority-Feminist Perspective on Women and Aging." *Journal of Women and Aging* 1(1/2/3): 195–216.

Haber, D., 1984. "Church-Based Programs for Black Care-Givers of Non-Institutionalized Elders." *Journal of Gerontological Social Work* 7(4): 43–55.

Johnson, H., Gibson, R. and Luckey, I., 1990. "Health and Social Characteristics: Implications for Services." In Z. Harel, E. McKinney and M. Williams, eds., *Black Aged.* Newberry Park, Calif.: Sage.

Miller, J., 1984. "Quilting Women." In M. Alexander, ed., *Speaking for Ourselves.* New York: Pantheon Books.

Preston, D., and Manfield, P., 1984. "An Exploration of Stressful Life Events, Illness, and Coping Among the Rural Elderly." *Gerontologist* 24(5): 490–94.

Sterne, R., Phillips, J. and Raushka, A., 1974. *The Urban Elderly Poor.* Lexington,

Mass.: D.C. Heath.

Taylor, J., 1986. "Religious Participation Among Elderly Blacks." *Gerontologist* 26(6): 630–35.

Taylor, J. and Chatters, L., 1986. "Church-based Informal Support Among Elderly Blacks." *Gerontologist* 26(6): 637–42.

CHAPTER TWELVE

Images of Home Death and the Elderly Patient

Romantic Versus Real

Andrea Sankar

Our current image of home death is informed by romantic notions of the past when, it was thought, families took care of their elderly better than they are cared for today. In these images, a dying elder is in his or her own bed, surrounded by devoted and caring family members. Often the dying person is articulate and alert enough to make deathbed pronouncements. In certain respects this picture is accurate and reflects a past in which women did assume the major care for the elderly and in which elderly people died mentally intact, often of short acute illness. In U.S. history (and in most nonindustrialized countries today) caring for the dying was very much a part of family life. From a young age children learned how to sit with the dying, tend to their needs, and comfort them. As the historian Emily Abel (1991) has shown, caring for the dying was an integral aspect of an adult woman's role in life throughout the early history of this country until the early part of the twentieth century. Women dressed wounds, nursed the dying person, and often acted as physicians, dispensing whatever medicines were available. Neighbors, friends, and relatives helped out with the nursing and with the woman's other responsibilities.

Care for the dying elderly changed about 50 years ago as advances in medical and nursing science offered the possibility that death could be delayed or prevented if a person received adequate care in a hospital. By the 1980s most deaths occurred outside the home. Pictures of death, except violent death, were subsumed by the efficient and effective image of modern medicine.

In recent years the move toward hospital death has been reversing. Several developments and events have come together to facilitate and encourage the reemergence of home death. These are (1) the popular movement to control one's own health and participate in care decisions such as assisted suicide, (2) the hospice movement, (3) a growing recognition of the limits of medical care, (4) improvements in home-based medical technology and pharmacology, and (5) changes in the insurance reimbursement for hospital stays. We need to understand how the dramatic technological and social changes of the last 50 years have affected the experience of home death. The image most people carry is outdated and in many cases seriously in error. It raises false expectations and inappropriate assumptions about what is involved and expected in a home death. This essay suggests a critical reappraisal of the romantic images of home death by describing current practices and issues.

FACTORS AFFECTING THE INCREASE IN HOME DEATH

The increase in home death is the result of various pressures that both pull and push people toward that option. Here are some of the "pull" factors:

Patient Control

Since the early 1970s a widespread movement in healthcare has encouraged patients and their families to assume more control over their health and the care they receive. Patient participation in decision making, informed consent, the holistic health movement, the women's health movement, and home birth are all examples of this move toward less paternalistic medicine and greater patient and family control over healthcare. Home death, which represents the desire of the dying person and the caregiver to assume control over the dying process, has been influenced by this trend.

Hospice

The formal acknowledgment of hospice treatment through reimbursement by Medicare and private insurance companies came about in the early 1980s. This official recognition has made it easier for people to die at home by providing them with some financial and professional support, by setting standards to regulate the professional care they receive, and by educating physicians, nurses, and the public about the home death alternative.

Limits of medicine

The limits of medical science are becoming clearer. Medicine's dramatic early successes in greatly reducing the number of deaths can largely be attributed to improvements in public health and advances in medicine's ability to treat infectious diseases (McKeown, 1979). In the future, it is unlikely that there will be equally dramatic breakthroughs in the cure of fatal illness. Instead, there will be a kind of fine tuning as medicine improves its ability to delay the onset of chronic disease, to keep chronically ill people alive longer, and to enhance the quality of life for those with chronic illness. Some argue that medical science has gone too far and that some high-tech treatments amount to an unnatural prolongation of life. Numerous high-profile cases concerning terminating life-sustaining technology have served to increase the general awareness of the limits of medicine for saving life in the seriously chronically ill. The increasing public awareness of the poor quality of life of those whose life must be sustained by high technology has led more and more people to forgo invasive or aggressive medical treatment to prolong life and to opt for palliative care, that is, care for pain and symptom relief, either in the hospital or at home.

The following are some pressures that might be considered "push" factors in the increase in home death:

Reimbursement

The prospective payment system, instituted in 1984, places financial constraints on the physician's ability to keep in the hospital a person who is not receiving active treatment. Further, there is a financial incentive to discharge patients as soon as possible.

Technological advances

At the same time that more people are choosing to die at home, advances in home-based medical technology and pharmacology are enabling people to return home who in the past would have had to remain in the hospital to receive treatment. These advances are especially important in the areas of pain control, oxygen therapy, intravenous treatments, nutritional supplements, and chemotherapy.

VARIETIES OF IMAGES AND PERCEPTIONS

In addition to the above factors, the HIV epidemic has helped to spur the move toward home death by advocating the empowerment of people with AIDS in decision making. They have led the way in showing that with the dramatic developments in home-based medical technology, it is possible for patients to live as well as die at home. Further, the financing crisis in healthcare will encourage, and may eventually require, arrangements whereby most deaths occur in a nonhospital setting.

THE EXPERIENCE OF CARING FOR THE DYING

Advocates of increased sensitivity to the dying process and the need for a noninterventionist approach to death tend to focus on the experience of the dying person. In this view there is a tendency to romanticize the process of home death as a highly preferable alternative to hospitalization. In evaluating this image, I do not wish to imply that a home death does not represent a powerful and moving experience for those involved. Rather, this romanticizing of home death is problematic because it tends to minimize how extremely difficult and strenuous the process can be. We cannot return to the past. Today home death is not the same as it was 50 years ago. The dying person is not the same and the caregiver is not the same.

People dying today tend to be dramatically sicker than they used to be (Gruenberg, 1977; Sankar, 1991b). This is so for several reasons. Because of the dramatic improvements in medical and nursing care, patients—those with HIV excluded—tend not to die of secondary diagnoses such as pneumonia or infections. Instead they survive to die from the primary disease itself, and as a result of our ability to keep people alive, by the time they do die, their bodies are severely compromised by the disease and thus very weak and debilitated. Another ironic result of improved healthcare is that people are older when they die. In many cases this means that, in addition to being sick, the dying person is very frail (Verbrugge, 1984). Both of these factors are important in a home death because they add to the responsibilities and level of care demanded of the family caregiver.

Caregivers too have changed. Women are no longer available to readily help one another in caregiving. Most work outside the home and many are single parents. Further, because of the trend toward hospital deaths in the last half-century, few potential family caregivers have experienced a death at home. Thus they are unable to step in and provide help with any ease and assurance.

The changed context combined with the lack of previous experience can make a home death a daunting task—one for which most people are not prepared. A more accurate image of a home death would include establishing the equivalent of an intensive care unit, sometimes accompanied by sophisticated medical technology, in one's home and placing the family on 24-hour call. Few caregivers are able to anticipate the intensity of this experience. Although hospice personnel do an excellent job of educating caregivers once they are in the home, the information and counseling available in the hospital about dying at home can be inadequate (Sankar, 1988). For example, caregivers are often not prepared for the extreme fragility of the dying person. With little firsthand experience, many caregivers imagine that dying is somehow a clearly defined, almost robust process, with a beginning and an end (Sankar, 1988, 1991b). Instead, dying is often a gradual process of steady decline. Even when it seems the person can decline no more and still remain alive, further losses are possible.

The patient continues to live throughout the process. This is the overwhelming benefit gained by people who have undertaken the responsibility for a home death—making the patient's death also a time of life. It also causes the most problems. Common actions and activities that people take for granted can become overwhelming problems and ordeals for the patient and caregiver. Eating; sleeping; taking a pill; drinking a glass of water; elimination; taking a bath; keeping the patient clean, turned, and free from bedsores; going outside—all represent major undertakings for the person and the caregiver. The fragility that can accompany age further complicates these efforts. Caregiving becomes helping the patient to live while he or she dies. To do this successfully from both the dying person's and the caregiver's perspective requires great attention to and inventiveness with the simplest tasks.

There are special problems faced by the dying person and caregiver, problems that do not simply represent amplifications and extensions of everyday problems but that are unique to the dying process. They may include anguish, anger, agitation, and fear on the dying person's part and crises and conflict between the caregiver and other family members. These problems can, of course, occur in a hospital setting, but there they tend to be somewhat contained by the fact that they are acted out in a strange and formal setting, one over which the participants have little control. This is not the case in the home. There the caregivers must deal directly with these problems and devise solutions as best they can.

The elderly may face special additional problems associated with the symbolic meaning of their death. Barbara Myerhoff (1978) has eloquently chronicled the special poignancy and melancholy of the Eastern European Jews who face death knowing that when they die, the last living witnesses to their vanished culture will be gone. Other anthropologists have documented similarly painful situations for the elderly (Amoss, 1981; Cool, 1981). But it is also the case that elderly people may have achieved a greater acceptance of death and thus escape the anger and denial sometimes present in younger people who are dying. The refusal or inability to accept death can cause significant caregiving problems.

A home death is a time when one sees both the best and the worst in a person. Despite traditional images of family harmony and togetherness, a home death can ignite serious strife within a family, and even lead to the dissolution of family ties. A dying person does not waste time on social gestures unless they express some deeper feeling. The rawness of the emotions, both positive and negative, may be overwhelming in a relationship already marked by strong ambivalence. In contrast to the hospital setting, in the home there are very few barriers to help control the emotional interactions. There are no, or few, strangers around, and the setting is one that usually belongs to or is deeply familiar to the patient. This is not a public space, and the conventions of public exchange often do not exist. Conversely, the very fact that a kind of truth exists is judged by those who have undergone the experience as one of a home death's greatest rewards.

THE CAREGIVER'S ROLE

Many caregivers who have gone through a home death experience feel it was the finest moment in their lives; they also characterize it as the most difficult and challenging thing they have accomplished (Sankar, 1991b). Two key qualities characterize the experience: the considerable responsibility that the caregiver must assume, and the physical and emotional stamina needed to undertake this task. Home death requires three main types of responsibility: decision making, speaking for the person or interpreting the person's wishes, and assessing the quality of the outside care. The extent to which the caregiver assumes these responsibilities depends on the dying person's own ability to make decisions. For some people, this remains intact until their deaths; for others, cognitive impairment clearly impedes decision making. Because the elderly are more vulnerable to disruptions in their environment and challenges to their physical beings, the potential cognitive problems caused by the dying process are likely to affect them.

The difficult situations (which are in the majority) are those in which the patient may be, and probably is, experiencing some degree of cognitive impairment, through (1) metastases to the brain characteristic of various forms of cancer, (2) dementia produced by a disease like Alzheimer's, (3) side effects or interactions of drugs, (4) malnutrition, or (5) severe depression. In these cases speaking on behalf of the dying person becomes much more difficult because the caregiver not only has to interpret what the patient cannot say but also has to assess whether what is said is actually meant. This is an extremely difficult area of care in hospitals as well as at home. Hospitals, however, often have the means to accurately assess the nature of the dying person's cognitive changes. Moreover, a hospital social worker is often available to help interpret to family members the dying person's wishes.

Interpreting the person's wishes in terms of social interactions involves decisions that may be less traumatic but are no less difficult or weighty. In situations where the family and close friends and associates may not be in harmony, which is sometimes the case, the caregiver may have to interpret the person's wishes concerning visiting, topics of conversation, and activities. Although the move from hospital to home represents an attempt to maintain and respect the dying person's autonomy, the caregiver's assumption of the right to make decisions can erode that autonomy. Struggles over autonomy and control can cause serious caregiving problems, especially when the dying person is no longer able to articulate his or her wishes.

In all these decisions, the caregiver and the dying person, if possible, have to weigh the needs of the living. Decisions made at a time like this are likely to affect the caregiver's future relationships to the people involved. Some situations are extremely difficult to handle.

Finally, the caregiver must assess the quality of the care being delivered to the home. Communities, agencies, and individuals within agencies differ. Community or agency care, although generally good, does vary in quality. Caregivers cannot assume that the services they are receiving are always appropriate. Caregivers sometimes find themselves having to supervise and assess the professional services they are receiving. This constitutes an added, and unnecessary, burden.

Caring for a dying person requires great emotional and physical stamina. Many dying people have great trouble sleeping. This insomnia can be caused by physical pain or mental anguish and fear. Unfortunately, drugs often do not provide adequate sedation. They may, in fact, have the opposite effect and stimulate the person. In addition, many dying people do not want to sleep. They say they do not need to sleep because they have so little time left; or they are afraid that if they go to sleep they won't wake up. Also, a person may require treatments that must be given throughout the night. Quality nighttime help is often the most difficult to obtain. Sleep deprivation over a long period is one of the most difficult problems for caregivers to resolve. In some cases it leads to rehospitalization of the patient just to enable the caregiver to get some sleep.

Caring for a dying person in the home affords little release from the tension. The home, ordinarily the refuge to which people escape from the worries and frustrations of life, becomes the concrete and immediate source of those worries. This is, of course, balanced by the fact that the dying person is at home. The ability to continue to live with the person while he or she dies is for many an adequate trade-off for the inability to find relief from the tension and pain of the dying process.

Providing homecare for a dying patient costs money. Insurance policies mainly cover skilled care, with minimal provision for a home health aide. The help of a home health aide who shares or takes responsibility for daily nursing tasks is particularly needed by caregivers. The caregiver may choose to provide all these services him or herself, but as the dying person becomes more acutely ill, more than one caregiver will be needed. Family and friends are often extremely valuable in providing this supplemental help, but it may mean that they must miss work and lose money. The hospice benefit in Medicare and private insurance is often not adequate to cover the care the person needs.

CONCLUSION

Improvements in medical technology combined with a need to reduce hospital costs have increased the trend toward home death. The nostalgia for a past where families were "more involved" in the care of the elderly can seriously distort people's expectations of what is involved in a home death. Home death is not something everyone should undertake. Adequate support for the caregiver, both professional and non-professional, is essential for a successful home death and also important for the well-being of the caregiver after the death has occurred (Bass, Bowman and Noelker, 1991; Sankar, 1991a). In the era of medical cost-containment and budget reduction, it is essential that home death not become simply a cost-saving measure.

Acknowledgments

Portions of this chapter have been adapted from the author's book, Dying at Home: A Guide for Family Caregivers (Johns Hopkins University Press).

References

Abel, E., 1991. *Who Cares for the Elderly: Public Policy and Experiences of Adult Daughters.* Philadelphia: Temple University Press.

Amoss, P., 1981. "Coast Salish Elders." In P. Amoss and S. Harrell, eds., *Other Ways of Growing Old: Anthropological Perspectives.* Stanford, Calif.: Stanford University Press.

Bass, D., Bowman, K. and Noelker, L., 1991. "The Influence of Caregiving and Bereavement Support on Adjusting to an Older Relative's Death." *Gerontologist* 31(1): 32–43.

Cool, L., 1981. "Ethnic Identity: A Source of Community Esteem for the Elderly." *Anthropological Quarterly* 54: 179–89.

Gruenberg, E. M., 1977. "The Failure of Success." *Milbank Memorial Fund Quarterly* 55: 3–24.

McKeown, T., 1979. *The Role of Medicine.* Princeton, N.J.: Princeton University Press.

Myerhoff, B., 1978. *Number Our Days.* New York: Simon & Schuster.

Sankar, A., 1988. "The Role of Caregiver–Physician/Nurse Communication in the Care of the Patient Dying at Home." Paper delivered at the annual meeting of the Gerontological Society of America, November.

Sankar, A., 1991a. "Ritual and Dying: A Cultural Analysis of Social Support for Caregivers." *Gerontologist* 31(1): 43–51.

Sankar, A., 1991b. *Dying at Home: A Guide for Family Caregivers.* Baltimore,

Md.: Johns Hopkins University Press.

Verbrugge, L. M., 1984. "Longer Life but Worsening Health? Trends in Health and Mortality of Middle-Aged and Older Persons." *Milbank Memorial Fund Quarterly* 62: 475–512.

CHAPTER THIRTEEN

Evolving Images of Place in Aging and 'Aging in Place'

Graham D. Rowles

Fashionable phrases in gerontology like "successful aging" and "continuum of care" have recently been supplemented by a new mantra—"aging in place" (Callahan, 1992; Tilson, 1990). The phrase has emerged in the context of a societal image of the desirability of growing old in a familiar environment. At the heart of this concept is a belief—a belief gradually being subsumed within public policy—that older people, particularly as they grow more frail, are able to remain more independent by, and benefit from, aging in environments to which they are accustomed. The benefits of residential stability are framed in sharp contrast to images of the stresses experienced by the need to relocate to progressively more supportive environments as frailty increases.

Implicit in the notion of aging in place as a policy priority is an assumption that the process of inhabiting a place, over time, somehow results in development of a distinctive sense of attachment that may be adaptive—and particularly so for older people. Recent studies have provided some support for this perspective (Boschetti, 1990; Rowles, 1983; Rubinstein, 1989, 1990). But none, to date, has directly sought to explore the way in which the growing body of research on the role of place in the experience of aging provides both an underlying rationale and, at the same time, the basis for critique of aging in place as an underpinning of contemporary elderly housing and social policy.

VARIETIES OF IMAGES AND PERCEPTIONS

In this chapter, I attempt to disentangle a number of themes within this issue by (1) summarizing an emerging body of writing on the way in which older people actually experience and develop affinity for the places of their lives, especially their homes; (2) tracing the link between this information and the historical emergence of aging in place as a philosophical focus of elderly housing and social policy; and (3) providing a critique of this focus in light of contemporary demographic and lifestyle trends that are leading to new forms of affiliation with place. Throughout the discussion, an underlying motif is the juxtaposition of *personal images*, largely implicit and taken for granted, of the relationship between self and place and a *societal image* of the nature of attachment to place that serves to guide public policy.

PLACE IN AGING

In order to understand the role of place in aging, it is necessary to consider the components of affiliation with the environments of our lives. First, we have a propensity to develop a physical attachment to place. There is a familiarity or sense of "physical insideness" that comes from inhabiting a location for an extended period (O'Bryant, 1983; Rowles, 1983). This is often taken for granted; we don't even think about it. But as, over the years, we become used to the configuration of our house, the path of our daily walk, and other familiar spaces, we develop a repetitive routine of use. We develop a "body awareness," an implicit preconscious sense of the setting that allows us to negotiate space without thinking and without coming to harm (Seamon, 1979). This type of "automatic pilot" is most apparent on those rare occasions when it breaks down; for example, when we bump into an object or trip over a throw rug in our home that has always been in the same location and that over several decades of residence has never previously constituted an obstacle. Such familiarity may even allow us to transcend apparent physiological and sensory limitations (Fogel, 1992, p. 16; Rowles, 1983). Paradoxically, it may also make us more vulnerable to small changes in the physical environment (for example, a child's toy left on the sidewalk or at the foot of the steps) that contribute to falls.

A second component of attachment to place is a sense of social affinity or "social insideness" that may evolve as a result of shared habitation. Home, for example, comes to develop a social identity as a place where certain rules of conduct and social norms apply. These emanate from a history of interactions with our family or living companions. There is our place at the table, the chair where grandpa always sits, a tradition of conversation at breakfast, of quietness in the early evening when the children study. The location develops a social rhythm and ambience that is acknowledged by its occupants; it becomes a social space. This phenomenon is familiar to all of us who have ever stayed at a friend's house and discovered how patterns of social interaction and the social aura of the place differ from that of our own home.

On a larger scale, we may develop similar social affinity with our neighborhood as a result of patterns of interactions with our neighbors and friends. Over the years, neighborhoods develop into social spaces with accepted social norms, expectations, and rules of behavior that are continually reinforced by residents—either formally, through organizations like neighborhood associations, or informally, through characteristic patterns of interactions among neighbors. Such patterns range from suburban over-the-fence or sidewalk conversations to the front stoop and street culture of some crowded inner-city neighborhoods. Individuals are enabled to develop a sense of "belonging" through participation in local culture and through sharing in and nurturing the neighborhood's sense of group identification with place.

A third component of attachment to place involves a critical temporal component and is intimately linked to our personal history. Our images of self and sense of identity as we grow older, and as those around us age, are inextricably intertwined with the places of our lives, the locations where the "grand fiction" of who we are has evolved over the duration of our existence (White, 1972). We remember our childhood homes, our room, the place where we used to play at the bottom of the garden or in the playground by the schoolyard. We remember where we used to "hang around" in adolescence—down by the park for the older generation, in the mall for those of more recent birth. We recall our days in college, or our first job, which molded the direction of our lives, on the fourth floor of an office building. There are the locations where we vacationed, the parks where our children played soccer or participated in Little League. Indeed, our lives involve a series of locations where significant events transpired.

As we grow older and remember the events of our lives, places are selectively recalled as we reinforce our image of who we are. As we accumulate layer upon layer of meaning within certain familiar loca-

117

tions like our home, these special places, themselves, come to assume a particular significance (Fogel, 1992; Rubinstein, 1989). They develop a time-depth and provide us with a sense of "autobiographical insideness" as they come to symbolize our identity—who we were and who we have become. Such intimate personal affiliation with particular places, especially with our home, may be adaptive. As we grow older, "remaining at home may have the additional significance of being the one constant in an emotional world threatened by losses" (Fogel, 1992, p. 16).

Our attachment to home, indeed the "creation" of this place, is nurtured and reinforced by the accumulation of artifacts and mementos— our furniture, a favorite picture, a treasured vase, the carpet we purchased on a European vacation, and our scrapbooks and the photographs of family that adorn the mantle (Boschetti, 1984; Csikszentmihalyi and Rochberg-Halton, 1981). Each item not only becomes a part of the contemporary place but also serves as a cue for the vicarious resurrection of and reimmersion in the places of our past. The result is that our home becomes an expression of who we are.

Although not exclusively an aging-related phenomenon, our ability to develop and maintain a sense of attachment to place, to sustain a sense of physical, social, and autobiographical insideness, and to organize the space within our home in a manner consistent with our needs and personality, may, as we grow older, become increasingly significant in preserving a sense of identity and continuity amidst a changing world (Boschetti, 1990; Rubinstein, 1989). As the literature on involuntary elderly relocation has suggested, abandoning these places may be associated with increased morbidity and mortality (Danermark and Ekstrom, 1990). In recent years these themes have emerged as part of the rationale for aging in place as the focus of residential and social policy.

AGING IN PLACE

The idea of aging in place as an underlying rationale for contemporary elderly housing policy has deep historical roots. It is embedded in the realities of rural and preindustrial America when mobility was limited and most people spent the duration of their lives in, or close to, the communities in which they were raised. It was not unusual for people to live and die in the dwelling in which they were born. Such residential inertia remains characteristic of the life histories of some of today's old-old (people 75 and above), particularly in parts of rural America. Not surprisingly,

118

it generates a strong sense of ownership and attachment to place.

Although the population became increasingly mobile during the early part of the twentieth century (in part as a consequence of the automobile and other transportation innovations), affiliation for place was given a new and somewhat different impetus by the explosion of homeownership and the growth of suburbia occurring after World War II. Between 1940 and 1960, owner-occupied units as a percentage of all occupied units increased from 43 to 62 percent (Callahan, 1992, p. 5). Increasingly, the image of success in American society became intertwined with aspirations of home-ownership. In a sense, what had been implicit became explicit. Several decades later, in 1988, this imperative and the legacy of success in achieving the American dream of a house in the suburbs resulted in 75 percent of the 19.5 million households headed by older persons being owner-occupied (AARP/AOA, 1989).

Not surprisingly, having achieved lifelong aspirations, the elderly tend to be reluctant to relocate. Despite a flurry of recent literature on elderly migration and a public image of a mass exodus of retirees from northern "snowbelt" states to Florida, Arizona, and other "sunbelt" states, the truth is that in comparison with the young, the elderly are far less mobile. Indeed, the *American Housing Survey* of 1985 indicated that in the previous year only 2 percent of elderly homeowners moved (U.S. Department of Commerce, 1985). That such stability extends to the remainder of the elderly population is reinforced by the fact that only 4 percent of the elderly population, homeowners or otherwise, relocated (Clark and Davis, 1990).

Given these historical trends, one would have thought that the idea of aging in place would have quickly and naturally emerged as the cornerstone of post–World War II housing and social policy. However, it appears that the reverse was the case. Indeed, during the 1950s, 1960s, and 1970s, the dominant image of aging in American society led policy makers (reinforced by gerontological theory) in a different direction. This was an era pervaded by the ethos of disengagement theory, a time when the image of the elderly as vulnerable and needy became deeply ingrained in public consciousness.

Two trends in particular served to reinforce this image. First, with the emergence of highly visible segregated housing options, "special" housing for the elderly became a significant component of the urban landscape. The title of Frances Carp's classic study of Victoria Plaza in

San Antonio, one of the first of these projects, *A Future for the Aged* (with its emphasis on the word "future"), is particularly revealing in this context (Carp, 1966). While the majority of older people continued to live in community settings, the proliferation of alternatives, particularly high-rise edifices in the central areas of large cities, began to convey an image of the elderly as somehow separate and in need of special services and housing arrangements. Indeed, this era was characterized by lively debates in gerontology on the relative merits of segregated versus integrated housing arrangements (Bultena and Wood, 1969; Rosow, 1967; Sherman, 1971). Even distinguished urban commentators, including Lewis Mumford, contributed to this debate (Mumford, 1953). Although the actual numbers of older people involved were small, the high visibility of the elderly high- rises conveyed an image that a normative pattern for the elderly was abandonment of their homes and movement into "supportive" settings where they could obtain types of assistance that were not available in their homes.

A second trend, reinforcing the image of the elderly as vulnerable and frail with a need to move to "special" environments, was the massive growth of the nursing home industry. A 1939 study by the Bureau of the Census counted 1,200 nursing homes with 25,000 beds (U.S. Senate, Special Committee on Aging, 1974). By 1960, this number had increased to 9,582 with 331,000 beds; and by 1970, there were more than 23,000 nursing homes with more than a million residents (1,099,412) (U.S. Senate, Special Committee on Aging, 1974). One aspect of this trend was the emergence of the image that nursing home residence was the normative final destination for the elderly. Even though only about 5 percent of the elderly population reside in nursing homes, and recent research suggests that less than half of the elderly population will ever utilize such facilities (Kemper and Murtaugh, 1991), an image of old age as a stage of life characteristically accompanied by relocation to special environments was reinforced.

Reflecting the ethos of the time, many of the housing and long-term-care options for the elderly assumed a willingness to relocate. Only in the past decade have we begun to acknowledge that the preference of the majority of the elderly continues to be the desire to age in place. Given our increasing understanding of the phenomenon of attachment to place and the historically grounded residential stability of the elderly, it should come as no surprise that a 1987 American Association of Retired

Persons survey revealed that 70 percent of older persons, especially women 80 years of age and older, agreed with the statement, "What I'd really like to do is stay in my own home and never move" (AARP, 1987).

With the rediscovery of aging in place as an underlying rationale has come a reorientation of the way in which residential and social policy regarding the elderly is conceived. First, there have been attempts to recast existing housing policy and support programs for the vulnerable and frail elderly within the rubric of a priority for aging in place. Pynoos (1990), for example, provides an inventory of more than 90 federal programs that he suggests are related to aging in place. He points out that currently many of these programs are not explicitly attuned to this underlying rationale. Many existing programs do not complement each other, and in addition they provide a poor framework for the development of a comprehensive aging-in-place-based support system for the vulnerable and frail elderly. Pynoos argues for more explicit concern with the implications of adopting aging in place as a policy priority. The recent proliferation of aging-in-place-oriented literature suggests some heeding of his advocacy (Callahan, 1992; Golant, 1992). Indeed, there is some evidence that aging in place has moved to center stage in policy debates.

The paradox here is that this adaptation may be occurring at a time when the role of place in aging may itself be changing and assuming new forms. It is important to acknowledge these changes if we are to develop aging-in-place-based policies that are fully attuned to the life experience and needs of present and future generations of the elderly.

EVOLVING IMAGES OF AGING IN PLACE AND PLACE IN AGING

As the idea of aging in place becomes more widely accepted as an underlying motif of public policy toward the elderly, it is important to critically evaluate some of the implications of the linkage between aging in place and place in aging. First, for many elderly people, the benefits of aging in place are entirely pragmatic. They have little to do with any sense of physical, social, or autobiographical attachment to place. Rather, for these people, aging in place is a high priority for reasons of cost and convenience. Although maintenance costs may increase, remaining in a dwelling that is owned, mortgage-free, in a location where one is fully aware of and integrated within a local service network and can receive practical assistance from friends and neighbors is a practical preference.

Second, not all older people are attached to a single place or set of places in the way described at the outset of this essay. There is a danger of romanticism—of exaggerating the role of familiarity and emotional affiliation with place as a component of residential preference. It also is possible to overstate the negative consequences of relocation for the elderly. For example, some elderly people who relocate, rather than revealing increased stress and morbidity, actually experience improved well-being (Kahana and Kahana, 1983; Savishinsky, 1991, pp. 79–85).

Third, the role of place in the experience of aging may be changing, indicating generational effects (Rowles, 1983). The current generation of the oldest-old (people over 85), particularly those residing in rural areas, have tended to be less mobile than the cohorts that are succeeding them. Their involvement within a single setting, or with a limited set of environments, is often longstanding. As a result, their level of physical, social, and autobiographical attachment to a single place is likely to be more intense. Length of residence is likely to have fostered a particularly strong relationship between such affinity and sense of self. Younger generations with a history of greater mobility have not had the time in a single location to develop such a strong affiliation. Their attachment to particular places, especially their homes, is likely to have less temporal depth and to involve a more diverse array of settings.

Fourth, it can be argued that our communications technology and progress toward an increasingly global society are such that we are moving toward new manifestations of relationship with place that are modifying the way in which we develop affinity with environments. Rather than developing affinities with unique locations, we are able to develop a comparable sense of familiarity and identification by involvement in places that are generic. For example, our neighborhood McDonald's may come to be an important location, physically, socially, and autobiographically. However, today we may visit what is in many respects the same place, the same McDonald's, in New York, Pittsburgh, Peoria, or even Moscow. There is a growing homogenization across environments. We can travel many miles and yet stay in a generic motel that enables us to feel a sense of the familiar. Essentially, global culture is moving toward a situation where every place can be anyplace in an essentially placeless world (Relph, 1976). Clearly, it is not possible to re-create the particular McDonald's where one stole one's first kiss, but place is increasingly becoming transferable. This, I would argue, has important implications not only for the role of place in aging but also for both the reality and the image of aging in place as the underlying focus of policy.

In sum, it would appear that both personal and societal images of the relationship between aging and place are evolving and assuming new forms. The role of place in our often implicit personal image of aging is changing. So, too, is the societal image of the meaning of aging in place. Ideally, one would hope for movement toward convergence of the two interrelated concepts.

What does this mean programmatically? Can we come up with suggestions that more fully acknowledge the link between the role of place in aging and the idea of aging in place as a rationale for policy? Not only must we more finely attune existing programs to aging in place (Pynoos, 1990), but we also must incorporate more explicit consideration of the role of place in aging into existing programs as well as in the creation of new ones. This can be accomplished by complementing the practical considerations, which have provided the rationale for contemporary aging-in-place philosophy, with recognition of the more subtle aspects of place in aging that are likely to enhance the success of such ventures. For example, acknowledging the potential for the transferability of a sense of place, it may be possible to develop programs that allow older people to retain at least a partial sense of aging in place even when physical relocation is unavoidable. Such programs might focus on facilitating the transfer of artifacts, photographs, and other memorabilia that are the cues to an individual's vicarious immersion in the places of their lives. They might involve prerelocation counseling that is sensitive to what is being given up in terms of a relationship with place. They may involve the sponsorship of reminiscence groups that provide a postrelocation social medium for the retention of a sense of continuing involvement in places that are physically abandoned. Most important, such efforts should be premised on attempts to ensure that separation from place does not become a separation from self. As we embrace a societal image of aging in place, we must not neglect the role of personal images of place in aging.

Acknowledgments

The author wishes to thank Beth Adkins and B. Jan McCulloch for helpful comments on an earlier version of this paper.

References

American Association of Retired Persons, 1987. *Understanding Senior Housing: An AARP Survey of Consumers' Preferences, Concerns and Needs.* Washington, D.C.: AARP.

American Association of Retired Persons/Administration on Aging, 1989. *A Profile of Older Americans.* Washington, D.C.: AARP.

Boschetti, M. A., 1984. "The Older Person's Emotional Attachment to the Physical Environment of the Physical Setting." (Ph.D. diss., University of Michigan).

Boschetti, M. A., 1990. "Reflections on Home: Implications for Housing Design for Elderly Persons." *Housing and Society* 17(3): 57–65.

Bultena, G. L. and Wood, V., 1969. "The American Retirement Community: Bane or Blessing." *Journal of Gerontology* 24(2): 209–17.

Callahan, J. J., 1992. "Aging in Place." *Generations* 16(2): 5–6.

Carp, F. M., 1966. *A Future for the Aged: Victoria Plaza and Its Residents.* Austin, Tex.: University of Texas Press.

Clark, W. A. V. and Davis, S., 1990. "Elderly Mobility and Mobility Outcomes." *Research on Aging* 12(4): 430–62.

Csikszentmihalyi, M., and Rochberg-Halton, E., 1981. *The Meaning of Things: Domestic Symbols and the Self.* Cambridge: Cambridge University Press.

Danermark, B. and Ekstrom, M., 1990. "Relocation and Health Effects on the Elderly: A Commented Research Review." *Journal of Sociology and Social Welfare* 17(1): 25–49.

Fogel, B. S., 1992. "Psychological Aspects of Staying at Home." *Generations* 16(2): 15–19.

Golant, S. M., 1992. *Housing America's Elderly: Many Possibilities/Few Choices.* Newbury Park, Calif.: Sage.

Kahana, E. and Kahana, B., 1983. "Environmental Continuity, Futurity, and Adaptation of the Aged." In G. D. Rowles and R. J. Ohta, eds., *Aging and Milieu: Environmental Perspectives on Growing Old.* New York: Academic Press, pp. 205–28.

Kemper, P. and Murtaugh, C. M., 1991. "Lifetime Use of Nursing Home

Care." *New England Journal of Medicine* 324:595–600.

Mumford, L., 1953. "For Older People—Not Segregation but Integration." *Architectural Record* 119(5): 191–94.

O'Bryant, S. L., 1983. "The Subjective Value of Home to Older Homeowners." *Journal of Housing for the Elderly* 1(1): 29–43.

Pynoos, J., 1990. "Public Policy and Aging in Place: Identifying the Problems and Potential Solutions." In D. Tilson, ed., *Aging in Place: Supporting the Frail Elderly in Residential Environments*. Glenview, Ill.: Scott, Foresman, pp. 167–208.

Relph, E., 1976. *Place and Placelessness*. London: Pion.

Rosow, I., 1967. *Social Integration of the Aged*. New York: Free Press.

Rowles, G. D., 1983. "Place and Personal Identity in Old Age: Observations from Appalachia." *Journal of Environmental Psychology* 3: 299–313.

Rubinstein, R. L., 1989. "The Home Environments of Older People: A Description of the Psychosocial Processes Linking Person to Place." *Journal of Gerontology, Social Sciences* 44(2): S45–53.

Rubinstein, R. L., 1990. "Personal Identity and Environmental Meaning in Later Life." *Journal of Aging Studies* 4(2):131–47.

Savishinsky, J., 1991. *The Ends of Time: Life and Work in a Nursing Home*. New York: Bergin and Garvey.

Seamon, D., 1979. *A Geography of the Lifeworld: Movement, Rest and Encounter*. New York: St. Martin's Press.

Sherman, S. R., 1971. "The Choice of Retirement Housing Among the Well Elderly." *International Journal of Aging and Human Development* 2(2): 118–38.

Tilson, D., 1990. *Aging in Place: Supporting the Frail Elderly in Residential Environments*. Glenview, Ill.: Scott, Foresman.

U.S. Department of Commerce, 1985. *American Housing Survey for the United States in 1985*. Current Housing Reports H-150-85. Washington, D.C.: Government Printing Office.

U.S. Senate, Special Committee on Aging, 1974. *Nursing Home Care in the United States: Failure in Public Policy*, Introductory Report. Washington, D.C.: Government Printing Office.

White, E. A., 1972. "Environment as Human Experience: An Essay" (M.A. thesis, Clark University, Worcester, Mass.).

Visual Images of Aging Women

Dena Shenk and Ron Schmid

A s an anthropologist/academic gerontologist and a documentary photographer, we have been engaged since 1987 in an ongoing project using photographic images of aging women to capture, study, and present the essence of the aging experience. The collaboration began as a final phase of the Rural Older Women's Project, an ethnographic study of the daily lives and systems of support of 30 rural older women in central Minnesota (Shenk, 1987, 1992). As part of the research, photographs were created of each of the women. These were then assembled in an exhibit, "Silver Essence: The Lives of Rural Older Women in Central Minnesota," which stands alone as an artistic endeavor and also has become an important component of the Rural Older Women's Project (see Figure 14.1).

The combination of the photographs with the research findings has served to foster a human connection—an awareness that these are real people. As one of the viewers of the exhibit observed: "The photographs take advantage of picturing the women in their own settings. The photos were so sensitive that the person in the setting made the story come to life. The result is very powerful and you get a picture of the person's lifetime. It is more than the sum of the two parts. Something very exciting happens" (Freshley, personal communication, 1989).

The photographic images are useful in two distinct ways. First, they stand alone as visual characterizations of aging women. By themselves, they tell us a great deal about the individuals portrayed. Second, in combination with the traditional research data, they provide a broader impact. They provide depth, detail, and "humanness" to what would otherwise be abstract, and they provide a vehicle for transmitting what has been learned to a larger audience. Viewers of the photos commonly say that they remind them of older people they know. In a sense, then, the photographs are not only images of specific individuals—they also generate reactions to themes and patterns within the aging experience.

Figure 14.1. Minnesota. Photograph by Ron Schmid. Used with permission, © R. M. Schmid, all rights reserved.

Figure 14.2. Croatia. Photograph by Ron Schmid. Used with permission,
© R. M. Schmid, all rights reserved.

VARIETIES OF IMAGES AND PERCEPTIONS

Based on the success of this endeavor, we decided to expand the photographic aspects of our work to include a look at other cultures. Our first efforts in this regard involved photographing older individuals in Dubrovnik and Zagreb, Croatia, during the summer of 1988. What was then Yugoslavia was selected because it offered some clear contrasts to the American Midwest and was also a site where the first author had done some preliminary research and had contacts.

There were obvious differences in the Yugoslavian effort compared to the original project. In Yugoslavia we had to work through translators, and our interactions were limited by the language barrier. We also had less time to spend with each subject. In Yugoslavia (and in the later phases of the project in Mexico and Costa Rica), less was known about the research subjects at the time the photographs were created; the photography and the interviews were done at the same time. The photographs in Dubrovnik and Zagreb show more of the setting and generally include more cultural artifacts.

A second photographic exhibit resulted. "Reflections on Aging: A Study from Yugoslavia and the U.S." is a comparative exhibit of aging in central Minnestoa and Croatia. Ten visual images of older women in Croatia were paired with ten photographs from central Minnesota, allowing the viewer to observe some of the similarities and differences (see figures 14.2 and 14.3). These images were matched according to visual themes that were dominant in the particular photographs. The exhibit includes a panel of explanatory text. Each photograph is marked simply "Yugoslavia" or "U.S."and the images are allowed to stand on their own with no further description. The visual themes of the matched pairs of photographs include a piano, a television set, and tapestry wall hangings as well as subjects reading, doing handicrafts, living with disability, in their kitchens, looking at old photographs, and showing their collections.

The next phases of the project were completed in Mexico in June 1989 and Costa Rica during the summer of 1990 (Shenk, Schmid and Stokes, 1991). Life history data were collected and photographs created of older adults in a range of social environments and economic situations.

A third photographic exhibit compares aging in Minnesota, Croatia, Mexico, and Costa Rica. "Portraits of Women: Images of Aging in Four Cultures" is composed of five images from each of the four countries, suggesting both similarities and differences in the aging experience in the four cultures (see figures 14.4 and 14.5, on page 139).

Figure 14.3. Minnesota. Photograph by Ron Schmid. Used with permission, © R. M. Schmid, all rights reserved.

131

Figure 14.4. Costa Rica. Photograph by Ron Schmid. Used with permission,
© R. M. Schmid, all rights reserved.

Figure 14.5. Mexico. Photograph by Ron Schmid. Used with permission,
© R. M. Schmid, all rights reserved.

VARIETIES OF IMAGES AND PERCEPTIONS

Our view of these images of aging women is through filters created by our own individual and cultural perceptions. An individual viewer's reactions to the photographs are based on previous experiences and perceptions of aging women. As these exhibits are displayed internationally, however, our efforts consistently receive strong support from professionals and the broader audience. There has been a common recognition of the similarity of patterns as well as differences in the aging experience in the various cultural contexts. A frequent response we receive is a desire to see more visual images incorporated into gerontological research.

Acknowledgments

This research was partially funded by the Central Minnesota Council on Aging, the St. Cloud State University Foundation and St. Cloud State University, Central Minnesota Initiative fund, Central Minnesota Arts Council, and Zapp Bank, St. Cloud, Minn.

References

Shenk, D., 1987. *Someone to Lend a Helping Hand—The Lives of Rural Older Women in Central Minnesota.* St. Cloud: Central Minnesota Council on Aging.

Shenk, D., 1992. "Someone to Lend a Helping Hand: Older Rural Women as Recipients and Providers of Care." *Journal of Aging Studies* 5 (4): 347–58.

Shenk, D., Schmid, R. and Stokes, E., 1991. "An Evolving Visual Methodology for Aging Research," paper presented at the Annual Scientific Meeting of the Gerontological Society of America, San Francisco.

Institutional Responses Over Time

Dispelling Ageism
The Cross-Cutting Intervention

Robert N. Butler

I t is increasingly within our power to intervene directly in processes of aging, with prevention, treatment, and rehabilitation. It is also within our power to intervene in social, cultural, economic, and personal environments, influencing individual lives as well as those of older persons en masse. If, however, we fail to alter present negative imagery, stereotypes, myths, and distortions concerning aging and the aged in society, our ability to exercise these new possibilities will remain sharply curtailed. Fortunately, we can treat the disease I call "ageism"—those negative attitudes and practices that lead to discrimination against the aged.

THE DISEASE

I originally coined the term "ageism" in 1968. As chairman of the District of Columbia Advisory Committee on Aging, I had been actively involved in the acquisition of public housing for older people. Stormy opposition arose against the purchasing of a highrise in northwest Washington. The causes for neighbors' negativism were intermixed, for not only were many of the future tenants black, they were also old and poor. In the course of a *Washington Post* interview, I was asked if this negativism was a function of racism; in this instance, I thought it more a function of ageism. As I originally defined it,

Ageism can be seen as a systematic stereotyping of and discrimination against people because they are old, just as racism and sexism accomplish this with skin color and gender. Old people are categorized as senile, rigid in thought and manner, old-fashioned in morality and skills. . . . Ageism allows the younger generation to see older people as different from themselves; thus they subtly cease to identify with their elders as human beings (Butler, 1969).

Not incidentally, in my original formula I was just as concerned with older people's negativism toward young people as I was with young people's negativism toward old people.

I saw ageism manifested in a wide range of phenomena, on both individual and institutional levels. These phenomena range from stereotypes and myths, outright disdain and dislike, and simple subtle avoidance of contact, to discriminatory practices in housing, employment, and services of all kinds. Negative images of "greedy geezers" and the "burden" of old age dependency abound in the mind, fueling the deprecation of all older people.

Lately, we have seen a rising chorus of voices further criticizing the aged, suggesting that they have had too many advantages. These views come from powerful quarters: politicians, scientists, and philosophers. Interestingly enough, however, these rumblings of intergenerational conflict are not the views of the people at large. National polls and surveys reveal just the opposite, that persons of all ages wish to see older persons keep their entitlements or even have them expanded. An excellent case in point is the spectacular rise of the long-term-care issue on the nation's agenda in both the halls of Congress and the recent presidential race.

In light of these surveys, which show that most people do not support intergenerational conflict but, rather, reaffirm the needs of older persons, how can we explain the continuation of the practice of ageism? On the one hand, I believe that the last decade has witnessed a steady improvement in the attitudes toward the aged, in part a consequence of general public education; increased media attention; the expansion of education in the community, colleges, and universities; and the continuing growth of gerontology. On the other hand, the success has been uneven. Residual pockets of negativism toward the aged still exist, most occurring subtly, covertly, and even unconsciously. Like racism and sexism, ageism remains recalcitrant, even if below the surface. Sensationalized caricatures make for good copy, even if they distort reality. But ageism can be—and has been—churned up from its latent position.

To ensure a reasonable place for older persons in society, we need to review some of these contemporary myths, stereotypes, and distorted facts in various institutional settings, which must be dispelled or reduced.

CURRENT MANIFESTATIONS

Unfortunately, even my own medical profession is not immune to ageism. Medical ageism is contracted in medical school. In fact, it was there that I first became conscious of prejudice toward age, there when I first heard the term "crock"—originally applied to patients with no organic basis for disease who were thought to be hypochondriacal—applied to middle-aged women and older people. Other terms abounded as well: "gomer" ("get out of my emergency room"); "vegetable"; and "gork" ("God only really knows" the basis of this person's many symptoms).

Medical schools do everything to enhance this virus. The first older person that medical students encounter is a cadaver. Fresh out of college, young people are confronted with death and their own personal anxieties about death, yet they are not provided with group or individual counseling. Not long after, they are exhausted from sleeplessness and subjected to hostility for not learning everything fast enough; by the time they are in their third or fourth year of medical school, they are ripe for cynicism. Then comes the internship, and they are working in excess of 80 hours per week, up in the middle of the night—and there is still one of those "gorks" to see.

Few medical school graduates enter the field of geriatrics. In fact, on the whole, physicians do not invest the same amount of time in dealing with elderly patients as they do with younger patients. Some doctors question why they should even bother treating certain problems of the aged; after all, the patients are old. Is it worth treating them? Their problems are irreversible, unexciting, and unprofitable.

Then too, ageism manifests itself in the hospitals themselves. A New York geriatrics professor, currently working at a hospital that, like others, is financially hemorrhaging, fears that his hospital will begin to view the elderly as quite unattractive once administrators see a recent report compiled by accountants tabulating the costs of each diagnosis-related group. Their report gave two tabulations—one for those over 70 and one for those under 70. They correctly concluded that the over-70 group costs the hospital more.

The severe cutback of services following the $750 billion tax cut inaugurated by the Reagan administration has brought steady criticism that Social Security and Medicare provide entitlements for older people yet deny them for the young. Newspapers report that the elderly's median income has risen significantly more that that of any other age group, basically because of Social Security benefits. From such distorted figures has emerged what Harold Sheppard has termed the "New Ageism," a dangerous viewpoint that envies the elderly for their economic progress and, at the same time, resents the poor elderly for being tax burdens and the nonpoor elderly for making Social Security so costly.

Daniel Callahan, expounding in Setting Limits (1987) the old-age-based rationing of healthcare originally suggested by former Colorado Governor Richard Lamm in 1983, sees older people as "a new social threat...that could ultimately (and perhaps already) do great harm." Programs that benefit the elderly, says Callahan, consume an ever increasing percentage of our taxes; healthcare expenditures, especially, are becoming extremely disproportionate and costly as the number of our elderly grows. We should use our money to help a sick child live rather than waste it on the old, who have already lived full lives.

It is noteworthy that this sense of renewed threat or concern about the number and proportion of older persons comes in a century of extraordinary increase in average life expectancy. Indeed, in the United States alone there has been a gain of 28 years of life expectancy since the year 1900, nearly equal to what had been attained over the preceding 5,000 years of human history. Eighty percent of this gain derives from marked reductions in maternal, childhood, and infant mortality rates. The remainder comes from reductions in death from heart disease and stroke. Although there is considerable chronic disease and disability at later ages, the expanding average life expectancy has yielded large numbers of increasingly vigorous, healthy, and productive older people.

Ageism may bear a relationship to the proportion of older persons in a society. A threshold that might be regarded as an achievement has, instead, become regarded as a burden. Ironically, the long-sought-for gain in life has been met by anxiety. What should have been a celebration has become a sense of threat. What should have been a message of hope has become a matter of despair.

Nations are afraid this increasing older population will become unaffordable, lead to stagnation of society's productive and economic growth, and generate intergenerational conflict.

TREATMENT

Georges Bernanos wrote, "The worst, the most corrupting lies are problems poorly stated." Let us then state these problems as they really are, putting various myths and distortions into their proper perspectives. In order to treat this disease, we first need to realize what is really true about older persons. One antidote to ageism is knowledge, the primary intervention.

If one asks more sophisticated questions related to the actual cost of old versus young, one must take care to look at all sources. When one looks only at federal expenditures, the old certainly receive more than the young. But in our system of government, we desire protection from the authority of the centralized state. Education, the great expenditure for the young, is not supported by the federal sector but rather on a community basis through property taxes. For example, in 1986, $140 billion of state and local moneys alone were spent on elementary and secondary public education in the United States. If the New Ageists would look at all the sources, they would see that a huge amount of money goes to children—as it should. A policy analysis of the cost of raising a child compared with the cost of caring for an older person still remains to be done.

Data do show conclusively that the condition of children as a group has deteriorated markedly, while that of older people, on the average, has improved. In fact, both children and the old living alone suffer from a 20 percent poverty rate. But the older people have not caused this deteriorating condition. That a society as rich as ours tolerates this suffering is abominable. It is important that the New Ageists realize and emphasize society's failure to deal constructively with the poverty of our children—but correction cannot be at the expense of the older people. We will not improve the welfare of children by tearing down what the elderly have impressively achieved. We need to support intergenerational programs, those that build a coalition between advocates for the children and advocates for the elderly.

One answer to the exploitation of intergenerational conflict has come with the founding of Generations United, which now includes the National Council on the Aging, the Child Welfare League of America, and all those marvelous mainstream organizations that have been advocacy groups for children. We must realize that we really are a

141

group of generations and we must work together, recognizing that today's older persons are yesterday's children and that today's children are tomorrow's elders. We must recognize that there is a continuity and unity to human life.

A VARIETY OF INTERVENTIONS

Another ageism intervention is the recognition that older people themselves are a market. Japan has the most rapidly growing population of older people in the world, as well as the highest life expectancy. When its Ministry of International Trade and Industry became excited by the "silver community concept"—establishing communities for their older citizens in other countries—there was considerable negative reaction in Japan. When Spain heard this plan, however, it pricked up its ears, for it saw this as a source of jobs. But if "silver communities" are economically valuable for Spain, then they are economically valuable for Japan itself— and for the United States. There is a lot of "gold in geriatrics," as the Wall Street Journal once wrote, when one considers capitalism as a necessary connection between producers and consumers.

Older persons themselves need to be productive and develop a philosophy on aging if we are to fight ageism.

Mastery is another important intervention. The simple ability of older people to have some control over their own lives will consequently become evidence to younger populations that the older population is not unproductive, depressed, disengaged, inflexible, or senile— myths that need to be dissipated in the attack on ageism.

Heavy investment in biomedical, behavioral, and social research is the ultimate cost-containment, the ultimate disease-prevention, and the ultimate service. When we eliminate Alzheimer's disease, the polio of geriatrics, we will empty half our country's nursing home beds. Spending money now will dramatically affect the image of senility and debility as inevitable in old age. Through research we can gain freedom from senility and further improvement in the strengthening of the social network that helps sustain people in grief. A better understanding of what accounts for the difference in life expectancy between men and women, and the development of a means to assist men to catch up with women by living longer, will do much to overcome many of the problems of age, as well as ageism.

CONCLUSION

From the social perspective, certainly, the treatment is to tap those sources responsible for maintaining a dignified and healthy old age. These include the individual, who should remain productive for as long as possible and be attentive to his or her health; the family, which, in fact, in the United States remains the most important caretaker of older persons; the community, which is rich with strong informal networks of friendly visitors and volunteers; and businesses.

Acknowledgments

This article is adapted, in part, from an essay by the same title that appeared in the Annals of the American Academy of Political and Social Sciences 503 (May 1989): 138–47.

References

Butler, R. N., 1969. "Ageism: Another Form of Bigotry." *Gerontologist* 9: 243–46.

Callahan, D., 1987. *Setting Limits:Medical Goals in an Aging Society.* New York: Simon & Schuster.

Sheppard, H., 1988. "The New Ageism and the 'Intergenerational Tension' Issue." Unpublished. International Exchange Center on Gerontology, University of South Florida.

The 'Graying' of the Federal Budget Revisited

Robert B. Hudson

o see that much has come to pass of what was predicted 15 years ago in an article about the consequences of growing public expenditures for the old leads to one of two conclusions: The author was a person of rare insight, or, it takes no genius to figure out that a snowball going down the side of a mountain might turn into something larger. But more important than the playing out of fairly predictable expenditure patterns are shifts that have occurred in our understanding of the place of the aged in public policy. "The 'Graying' of the Federal Budget and Its Consequences for Old Age Policy" (Hudson, 1978) anticipated important changes in the perceptions, politics, and policies of aging, but not always in the shape or of the magnitude that was to later emerge.

THE SCENE

Several trends predicted in "Graying" have largely materialized. Federal expenditures directly and indirectly benefiting the elderly have grown significantly in both absolute and relative terms. Aging agencies find themselves under unprecedented bureaucratic pressures as "problems" associated with an aging population have gained growing recognition at federal and state levels. Pressures from competing social welfare constituencies have emerged, and the rise or recognition of new social issues such as those concerning persons with AIDS or single-parent families have markedly increased. Most troublesome of the anticipated trends has been widespread reinterpretation of policy successes in aging as policy excesses in which the aged find themselves transformed into an overindulged and singularly greedy population.

These forecasts can be viewed as insightful only if one recalls the prevailing ethos in political gerontology when the article was written. Primary attention was focused on further extending the new-found policy gains of older Americans in a range of areas: income, healthcare, housing, community-based social services, among others. At the time, however, there was considerably less appreciation of the budgetary implications of the policy accomplishments of the 1965–74 decade: escalating hospital and physician costs following enactment of Medicare, a rapid expansion of the nursing home industry generated in large part by the Medicaid program, four double-digit benefit increases in Social Security between 1968 and 1972, purchasing power guarantees added through cost-of-living adjustments in 1974, guaranteed minimum benefits for poor elders through the new Supplemental Security Income program, major housing subsidies through the Section 202 and Section 8 programs, and the expansion of community-based care assured by the creation of a nationwide network of aging agencies. There was, as well, broad-based denial in aging and other advocacy circles of the sobering impact being produced by a series of secular events of the time. Economic problems centered on oil shocks, inflation, and limited income growth, and an emerging crisis in public sector authority brought on by Vietnam, Watergate, and weak presidential leadership were adding low public morale to the growing concern about escalating costs.

THE PERSPECTIVES

"Graying" was born of two prominent schools of thought in political studies. The first centered on political culture and the role of prevailing values in accounting for the prominent place of the aged in the enactment of "breakthrough" policies in American social welfare. The original Social Security legislation of the 1930s, the passage of Medicare, and welfare reform for "the adult categories" through SSI's enactment were each featured cases in and exposition of how expansion of social programming centered largely or exclusively on the old. In the American "opportunity-insurance state" (Marmor, Mashaw and Harvey, 1990), there was a lower policy threshold for the old than for working-age groups and even children.

"Graying" went on to warn that this singular legitimacy long enjoyed by the aged was coming under unprecedented pressure. Public perceptions were changing in light of the realization that not all of the old were destitute and ill and that much attention had been paid to their concerns in recent years. That has proven partially to be the case, but the article did not fully anticipate the segmentation of views about aging policy that developed between the public and opinion makers. In the latter circles, there has been a wholesale fracturing of elders' political legitimacy. Despite continuing strong public support for the old, the days are gone when one might contend—as "Graying" noted had historically been the case—either that elders' legitimacy "obviates the need for power" or that elders possess a "political utility" enabling them to serve as the lead constituency in the development of populationwide program coverage. Broader concerns about economic growth and the well-being of today's young have diluted the notion that the aged can be regarded as a singularly protected population or one that can serve to break down ideological barriers.

The article's second perspective centered on "constituency-building" activities of the organized old. It built on Binstock's (1972) application of "interest group liberalism" (Lowi, 1969) to the field of aging, wherein organized interests are understood not to compete and compromise with each other but rather to form self-contained fiefdoms comprising public and private officials pursuing mutually supportive agendas. In a world of "iron triangles," private sector interests, sympathetic legislators, and responsive administrators were in position to provide on a reciprocal basis the service contracts, political support, and legislative authorizations needed by the respective parties.

"Graying" went on to argue that the structural elements necessary for interest group liberalism to thrive were clearly beginning to erode. Tight budgetary times and growing demands for service brought heretofore "subgovernmental" (Cater, 1964) activities to the attention of major outside actors—spenders and savers alike. On the spending side, competition between groups was reintroduced as dollars became tight. On the savings side, previously separate authorization and appropriation decisions were consolidated and made in massive and singular strokes—most notably, the 1981 Omnibus Budget and Reconciliation Act.

NEW DIMENSIONS IN AGING POLITICS

Two constructs used to characterize the structure of decision-making arenas—"scope of conflict" and "organization of bias" (Schattschneider, 1960)—speak directly to what has happened to aging-related politics since circa 1978. Scope of conflict refers to the extensiveness and presumed diversity of those engaged in the decision-making process, and organization of bias captures the collective orientations of those involved. What has happened in aging policy over 15 years is that the scope of conflict has broadened immeasurably, and the "bias" in the organization of aging-related politics has shifted along several dimensions. On the matter of scope, there may be no better policy example than aging for illustrating Schattschneider's dictum that "the outcome of the political game depends on the scale on which it is played" (p. 20). The bias in aging-related policy may be seen as having evolved from the common currency of 20 years ago centered on "the aging and society" to today's greater awareness that "the aging" are increasingly about multiple ages, races, generations, and classes. The changing "rotation" of the scope and bias of aging policy can be seen in at least three arenas.

From Distribution to Dedistribution

We have seen the passsage of an earlier time in which an expanding economy, sympathetic images, and domain consensus among interest groups could bring "no pain" policy gains for elders. Concern with costs, trade-offs, and efficiency have increasingly supplanted an earlier era's emphasis on access, opportunity, and expansion. A critical corollary to social issues being more hotly contested has been a decided broadening of arenas in which hard choices were being made.

The evidence for this transformation is seen most clearly in the case of Social Security. In the course of one decade, significant liberalization was supplanted by unprecedented tax increases and notable benefit reductions. In 1972, no less a hard-headed fiscal realist than Wilbur Mills, chair of the House Ways and Means Committee, called for a 20 percent increase in Social Security benefits. And, in an ironic final chapter to Social Security's expansionary phase, Republican lawmakers succeeded, as an economy measure, in having future benefit increases tied to the cost of living. By 1983, the National Commission on Social

Security Reform, including no less a stalwart of the program than Robert Ball, found itself taxing benefits, delaying cost of living adjustments, and instituting a higher eligibility age for full Social Security benefits. In Light's (1985) words, we had gone from distribution to "dedistribution," a world of negative-sum politics where everyone loses.

Perhaps more telling than the substantive changes in Social Security law was the shift in venue for making decisions about Social Security. For a 30-year period after the enactment of the original legislation, Social Security policy was effectively made by a handful of key players in Congress and the Social Security Administration (Derthick, 1979). Meetings of the Trustees were largely pro forma, changes in law and regulation—with occasional exception such as addition of disability and health insurance—were incremental and noncontroversial, and the public's "take" on Social Security was a mixture of great support and low salience.

The unannounced coming of a "crisis" and the need to impose a "dedistributive" solution in a program as massive and presumptively secure as Social Security shattered existing understandings about Social Security policy-making. It was not surprising that difficult choices would move decision making from the cloakrooms of Washington, but ordinarily, emerging differences would be settled through a more inclusive process in Congress and the executive branch. Attempts to do so failed repeatedly in the early 1980s, with both parties petrified by fear of touching Social Security, the so-called "third rail of American politics." Needed decisions were kicked to a bipartisan commission charged with bearing the burden of distributing the pain. Formal enactment of the commission's recommendations was rushed through Congress in lockstep fashion, no one willing to remove even a brick from the facade.

In a decade, the politics of Social Security went from broad-based interest in liberalizing benefits to near abdication of responsibility for making hard choices. From everyone wanting in (Mayhew, 1974), everyone now wanted out (Light, 1985).

From Age Toward Class

Traditional views of the aging have been challenged and reconstructed over the past 15 years. As the perceived homogeneity of the old has declined, so has their singularity as a policy constituency. Initially, the change in perception was a matter of a widening appreciation of what much of social gerontology had long been saying: The old are a het-

149

erogeneous population. The next step was the gradual recognition that there were troublesome policy implications in this newly acknowledged heterogeneity. At once, the old seemed to be healthy and frail, rich and poor, isolated and integrated. Nor was there anything random about how these qualities were distributed; there was marked "colinearity" along key indicators of well-being—income, health status, social integration.

More recently yet, a growing literature under the rubric of diversity and aging has made clear differential patterns of late-life well-being attributable to gender, race, and class. The most encompassing analysis of this stratification of the old—its extent, its origins, and its conse-quences—was found in the political economy of aging literature also emerging during the 1980s (Estes, Swan and Gerard, 1982; Olson, 1982; Graebner, 1981). Class analysis found the aged to be a population dis-missed, used, and manipulated by concentrated capital—to have become a twentieth century addition to the class of the oppressed.

In the more proximate political arena, the role of class is seen on sever-al fronts. The taxation of Social Security benefits for higher income elders was the first major step in this direction, implicitly recognizing that amount of income was a better indicator of well-being than assumptions about the purposes of income from different sources. At a more modest level, moves toward targeting of benefits and cost-sharing under the Older Americans Act are reflective of the same concerns. Targeting represents class issues on the benefit side—those who demonstrably need should receive. Cost-sharing represents class on the financing side—those who wish services and have the means should pay at least part of the freight.

The new place of class in aging-related policy was put in yet starker relief in the case of the Medicare Catastrophic Care Act (MCCA). The role of class is seen both in the thinking of the act's sponsors and in the actions of that part of the beneficiary class that led to the act's repeal. In the first instance, the imposition of a surtax on higher income elders to fund bene-fits represented a sharp break in both the logic and understanding of Medicare financing. No longer were elders considered a homogeneous group for insurance purposes; now there would be formal recognition that some could afford to pay more for the same range of benefits than could others. In the second instance, the better-off banded together in rejecting a tax scheme they saw as patently unfair. Not only were they being asked to pay more for the same, they were being told to pay for pro-tections that they had already secured through the private sector. For some elders, needs were not present and insurance was not wanted.

From Ages to Generations

MCCA also serves as Exhibit A in the newfound policy concern with equity between generations. It was the Reagan administration's stricture that any new Medicare benefit package be financed by elders themselves—a law, in Senator Durenberger's words, that "would not penalize one generation for the sake of another" (Quadagno, 1989)—that precipitated imposition of the surtax. The costs of MCCA's final benefit package, now including prescription drug and spousal asset protection features, created intolerable pressures on the only available elder-only financing mechanism, the Medicare Part B premium.

The generational equity movement raises a number of important questions for aging-related policy. Most directly, it forces attention on whether the half-century-old notion of a compact between the generations is either fair or, in fact, operative. Generational redistribution presumes that the aggregate circumstances of different generations will be roughly the same so that the "generational accounting" (Kotlikoff, 1992) balances. There is now clearly reason to question that assumption, our having seen in this time span a "Depression generation" (b. 1900–1920); a "golden cohort" (b. 1936–1945); a two-wave baby boom (b. 1946–1954; 1955–1964), and a baby bust (b. 1965–1984), each cohort's life chances being constrained in different ways. Most topical today is contrasting what are generally seen as tough life prospects for those born in the final quarter of this century with the cohort born roughly between the two World Wars. These individuals are described by David Thomson (1989) as a "welfare generation," one which "aged" in conjunction with the welfare states of the industrial world over the second half of this century.

In stark contrast to these analyses are those of observers who see the generational equity movement to be about neither generations nor equity. In tracing the rise of Americans for Generational Equity (AGE), Quadagno (1989) argues that the movement was centrally about privatization and, in that vein, sees the MCCA as "the first successful attempt to desocialize an entitlement program." She and many others noted that beyond being members of what is arguably a disadvantaged generation, AGE's key staffers were white, male, and decidedly middle class, attributes that easily rival generation in their saliency. Quadagno made these comments at a time and in a place (the progressive journal,

Politics and Society) where it could be taken as at least mildly incendiary. Today, one doubts that Peter Peterson, Paul Tsongas, or Warren Rudman (founders of the so-called Concord Coalition, a supraestablishment successor to AGE) would quibble with that characterization, seeing entitlements that are out of hand, bleak prospects for today's young, and an economy starving for investment capital.

AGE, CLASS, AND GENERATION

Age is not the political variable it was at the time of "Graying." That today's old are a large and growing group with a range of needs and in receipt of a host of benefits is not in dispute. "Graying" anticipated the growing diversity of the old and the growing mismatch that would evolve between need and receipt. But it did not fully foresee the break between elite and mass opinion concerning age-based programs nor the degree to which income-related changes would be introduced into the financing of major aging programs.

Shattschneider's scope and bias dimensions are particularly useful in capturing the structural changes that have taken place in aging-related politics. The scope has been massively transformed, with aging issues of such budgetary and symbolic significance that they are increasingly viewed in contentious, redistributive terms. Changes in the bias are more variegated, revolving around how to understand the place of people who are old at different points in time. But one no longer asks in straightforward fashion simply about the differences between the old and other members of society. From the added perspective of both class and generation, one asks about the within-group differences and the between-group similarities of the aged and others. The issue is no longer that the population and budget are graying; the issue today is how to sort out the increasingly visible salt and pepper striations.

References

Binstock, R. H., 1972. "Interest Group Liberalism and the Politics of Aging." *Gerontologist* 12(2): 265–80.

Cater, D., 1964. *Power in Washington.* New York: Random House.

Derthick, M., 1979. *Policymaking for Social Security.* Washington, D.C.: Brookings Institution.

Estes, C. L., Swan, J. H. and Gerard, L.W., 1982. "Dominant and Competing Paradigms in Gerontology: Toward a Political Economy of Aging." *Ageing and Society* 2(2): 151–64.

Graebner, W., 1981. *A History of Retirement.* New Haven, Conn.: Yale University Press.

Hudson, R. B., 1978. "The 'Graying' of the Federal Budget and Its Consequences for Old Age Policy." *Gerontologist* 18(5): 428–40.

Kotlikoff, L. J., 1992. *Generational Accounting.* New York: Free Press.

Light, P., 1985. *Artful Work.* New York: Random House.

Lowi, T. J., 1969. *The End of Liberalism.* Boston: Norton.

Marmor, T. R., Mashaw, J. L. and Harvey, P. L., 1990. *America's Misunderstood Welfare State.* New York: Basic Books.

Mayhew, D. R., 1974. *Congress: The Electoral Connection.* New Haven, Conn.: Yale University Press.

Olson, L. K., 1982. *The Political Economy of Aging.* New York: Columbia University Press.

Quadagno, J., 1989. "Generational Equity and the Politics of the Welfare State." *Politics and Society* (17)3: 353–76.

Schattschneider, E. E., 1960. *The Semi-Sovereign People.* New York: Holt.

Thomson, D., 1989. "The Welfare State and Generation Conflict:Winners and Losers." In P. Johnson and D. Thomson, eds., *Workers and Pensions.* New York: St. Martin's Press.

CHAPTER SEVENTEEN

Representations of Aging in Contemporary Literary Works

Robert E. Yahnke

In one of his journals, John Cheever (1991) summarized the strengths of literary works to convey a myriad of themes and images of human experience. He wrote of literature as having a unique and compelling power to reveal the condition of humanity:

> To disguise nothing, to conceal nothing, to write about those things that are closest to our pain, our happiness; to write...about the foolish agonies of anxiety, the refreshment of our strength when these are ended; to write about our painful search for self...to write about the continents and populations of our dreams, about love and death, good and evil, the end of the world (p. 32).

Cheever's ideas are applicable as well in the context of literary representations of aging. Literary works offer a point of entry for readers who are interested in expanding their understanding of old age. Through literature, readers come to know the untranslated, uninterpreted experience of the old. Readers are challenged to make some sense out of the idiosyncracies, complexities, ambiguities, and contradictions of these representations of life in old age.

Achenbaum (1989) acknowledged the power of literary works to provide the context for instructive life lessons relating to gerontological education: "What seems to have fascinated writers everywhere throughout the ages is the insistence of the old to remain true to—to (re)affirm—the basic truths of the human condition in their simple utterances, in their seemingly pedestrian gestures, and in their very mien" (p. xx). Achenbaum's reference to "basic truths of the human condition" reflects at once the universality of representations of aging in literature and the various means by which literary artists individuate characters in old age, depict their inner lives, portray their interactions across generations, their friendships and their loves, and the basis of their relationships with family and friends.

This article examines some of the ways in which contemporary literary artists have represented aging. Three enduring themes will be surveyed: the mutual benefits of intergenerational relationships, especially as those relationships involve issues in caregiving; the dimensions of intimate relationships in old age; and the portrayal of age as a time of creative tension and delicate balancing between complementary, opposing forces encountered in later life. For the purposes of this article, examples from two literary forms, novels and memoirs, will be used to illustrate these themes. But additional examples could be found in stories, poems, and plays, many of which are anthologized in three recent texts, *Full Measure: Modern Short Stories on Aging* (Sennett, 1988), *Songs of Experience: An Anthology of Literature on Growing Old* (Fowler and McCutcheon, 1991), and *Literature and Aging: An Anthology* (Kohn, Donley and Wear, 1992).

Intergenerational relationships represent a persistent theme in the literature of aging. In many contemporary literary works, the theme of intergeneration has been associated with problems of caregiving. These works provide insights into the emotional and psychological effects of caregiving on the caregivers. Having the capacity to make connections outside one's own cohort may be a remarkable, life-affirming achievement; at the same time, it may lead to strained, even frustrating family ties when caregiving is involved. In Philip Roth's memoir *Patrimony* (1991), for example, a son's obligations of caregiving for his father generate a complex set of interactions that are not easily resolved. Roth highlights the confusion, ambivalence, and even hostility of the middle-aged caregiver who is forced to contend with circumstances he has never been prepared to face. In this memoir the son realizes eventually the implications of the term "patrimony" and its meaning in the context of his relationship to his father.

Art Spiegelman's two books, *Maus: A Survivor's Tale*, I and II (1986,

1991), combine the subjects of Holocaust survivors and family history in the context of an unusual format—comic book art. The father-son relationship depicted in these books reveals additional insights into the nature of intergenerational relationships, especially as they are complicated by caregiving needs. The life lessons in these texts revolve around Spiegelman's attempts to provide adequate caregiving for his father, who suffers from a heart condition, and the son's inquiry into his father's experiences at Auschwitz. The father's detailed recollections of how he survived the concentration camp reveal the remarkable strengths of character and will he possessed during those trying years. But the old man who stands before his son now seems a shadow of that former self: He exhibits spiteful, racist, self-centered, and defeatist behaviors that appall his son. But Spiegelman suggests that through the hours of conversation with his father and through the give-and-take of the caregiving role he has assumed, the son is reacquainted with his father and learns to accept the basis of this newfound relationship.

The intergenerational relationship in Pat Barker's novel *The Century's Daughter* (1986) is based upon a quick warmth and fondness felt by the young social worker and the old woman he befriends. In some respects the caregiving flows back and forth between the older woman and the younger man. The caregiving relationship in Clyde Edgerton's *Walking Across Egypt* (1988) is directed even more from the old to the young. In this novel an elderly widow combines her culinary talents, her faith, and her social and interpersonal skills to redeem the life of a wayward teenager.

All these sources suggest that literary writers view problems of caregiving in the larger context of questions about human character and the basis of significant relationships between individuals. In these works, caregivers may be changed, and even transformed, by their interactions with another generation; or both parties to the intergenerational relationship may discover mutual benefits based upon their interaction.

A second theme in contemporary literary works is demonstrated by writers who provide insights into intimate relationships between older people. Readers of Pat Barker's *Union Street* (1983) will never forget the sexual encounter between an aging prostitute and a recently retired man. Blonde Dinah is a splendid image of old age, a "brassy blonde," symbol of sexual power, still active and engaged in life, and each night facing with equanimity whatever prospects she encounters. Other rela-

157

tionships in old age emphasize the longstanding intimacy between older adults. A good example is the relationship between Joe and Ruth Allston in Wallace Stegner's *The Spectator Bird* (1976). Joe Allston, 70, has spent a lifetime searching for a "safe place," a sanctuary from various emotional scars. Stegner portrays a couple whose relationship has become that safe place: Joe and Ruth are comfortable with each other, and they know how to "read" the other's moods. Their repartee, their love of reading, their ability to complement each other's idiosyncrasies, and their ability to relive emotionally painful memories and face the rest of their old age together are the ingredients of their particular intimacy.

Another memorable older couple is Gemma and Rupert, both in their 70s, in Hortense Calisher's *Age* (1987). Both keep separate diaries, and the structure of the novel moves back and forth from one person's account of daily living to the other's. Along the way, this couple consider what is promising as well as threatening in their future. Their intelligence, wit, companionship, sexuality, and individuality are expressed throughout the novel. Other literary works, like *Spence + Lila*, a novel by Bobbie Ann Mason (1988), and *Only Yesterday*, a novel by Julian Gloag (1986), provide further instances of intimate relationships that are founded on strength of character and mutual affection.

A third theme is represented in literary works that portray old age as a time of unceasing ebb and flow of complementary, opposing forces: hate and love, fear and courage, disengagement and engagement, despair and hope, and so forth (Yahnke and Eastman, 1990). These oppositions reflect a spectrum of emotional and psychological responses to aging. Within the category of hate, for instance, characters may respond with anger, hostility, jealousy, grudges, selfishness, and even self-loathing.

Within the category of love, characters may respond with devotion, forgiveness, respect, compassion, acceptance, sacrifice, reconciliation, and friendship. Florida Scott-Maxwell (1968) wrote, "The crucial task of old age is balance, a veritable tightrope of balance; keeping just well enough, just brave enough, just gay and interested and starkly honest enough to remain a sentient human being" (p. 36). In these literary works, older characters are concerned with finding some sense of balance—some means of functioning—between the opposing pairs of categories so that they may survive the ongoing dynamism of their life circumstances.

The perils of not finding that sense of balance in old age are well represented in Kazuo Ishiguro's *The Remains of the Day* (1989). In this novel, an aging butler completes a six-day motor trip to the west of England in the 1950s. Of course, the literal journey he makes is paralleled by a spiritual journey that reveals the psychological, and even spiritual, crisis he faces in his impending old age. Ishiguro creates a character who is disabled by conflicting forces of emotion versus restraint, risk taking versus a self-enforced "dignity," and commitment to relationships versus disengagement and solitude.

Other literary works convey similar instances of older individuals struggling to maintain their balance, confronting inevitable turning points in their lives. Howard Kohn's memoir of his father, *The Last Farmer* (1989), portrays a man who forestalls the inevitable loss of the family farm for many years. Eventually he yields to changing economic patterns and sells the farm. But he learns to adapt to his retirement and finds a measure of happiness by traveling with his wife and visiting their extended families. The old woman in Jessica Anderson's *Tirra Lirra by the River* (1978), after facing a difficult life of loneliness and self-denial, and after reviewing her life and choices made and not made, is also able to contemplate her old age with a measure of resolution, and even equanimity. But that sense of balance in her life comes only after a painful process of introspection and engagement.

One of the main characters in Pat Barker's *Union Street* (1983) is an old woman, hobbled by the wreckage of her body and fearful of life in an institution. Feeling abandoned by her family and angry at her impersonal treatment at the hands of the social service agency, the old woman struggles to retain a sense of security and dignity in her life. Unable to maintain herself in her small apartment after a stroke partially disables her, she walks to a park one cold winter day and ends her life asleep on a park bench. Barker is careful to portray this, not as an act of resignation or despair, but as a defiant act through which the old woman declares her individuality and identity in the face of the complementary forces of hope and despair.

The stories told by these literary artists express a variety of representations of the aging experience. Their power to characterize the inner lives of older individuals, portray the contradictions inherent in intergenerational relationships, and reveal the dynamics of intimate relationships in old age is a sign that contemporary literary artists are committed to an honest and probing exploration of what it means to be old. Robert Coles, in *The Call of Stories: Teaching and the Moral Imagination* (1989), characterized the means by which literary works provide insights into the human condition:

> The whole point of stories is not "solutions" or "resolutions" but a broadening and even a heightening of our struggles—with new protagonists and antagonists introduced, with new sources of concern or apprehension or hope, as one's mental life accommodates itself to a series of arrivals: guests who have a way of staying, but not necessarily staying put (p. 129).

The literary works examined in this chapter reflect the depth and range of experiences in old age, as well as the intensity with which readers can identify with the old as they are portrayed in literary works. All of these literary works affirm the contradictions, complexity, and uncertainty that lie at the heart of the experience of aging.

Bibliography

Achenbaum, W. A., 1989. "Foreword:Literature's Value in Gerontological Research." In P. Bagnell and P. S. Soper, eds., *Perceptions of Aging in Literature: A Cross-Cultural Study.* Westport, Conn.: Greenwood Press.

Anderson, J., 1978. *Tirra Lirra by the River.* New York: Penguin.

Barker, P., 1984. *The Century's Daughter.* London: Putnam.

Barker, P., 1986. *Union Street.* New York: Putnam.

Calisher, H., 1987. *Age.* New York: Weidenfeld & Nicolson.

Cheever, J., 1991. "Journals: From the Sixties—I." *New Yorker* 66 (Jan. 21): 28–63.

Coles, R., 1989. *The Call of Stories: Teaching and the Moral Imagination.* Boston: Houghton Mifflin.

Edgerton, C., 1988. *Walking Across Egypt.* New York: Ballantine Books.

Fowler, M., and McCutcheon, P., 1991. *Songs of Experience:An Anthology of Literature on Growing Old.* New York: Ballantine Books.

Gloag, J., 1986. *Only Yesterday.* New York: Henry Holt.

Ishiguro, K., 1989. *The Remains of the Day.* New York: Vintage Books.

Kohn, H., 1989. *The Last Farmer: An American Memoir.* New York: Harper & Row.

Kohn, M., Donley, C., and Wear, D., eds., 1992. *Literature on Aging: An Anthology.* Kent, Ohio: Kent State University Press.

Mason, B. A., 1988. *Spence+Lila.* New York: Harper & Row.

Roth, P., 1991. *Patrimony.* New York: Simon & Schuster.

Scott-Maxwell, F., 1968. *The Measure of My Days.* New York: Penguin.

Sennett, D., 1988. *Full Measure: Modern Short Stories on Aging.* St. Paul, Minn.: Graywolf Press.

Spiegelman, A., 1986. *Maus: A Survivor's Tale, I: My Father Bleeds History.* New York: Pantheon.

Spiegelman, A., 1991. *Maus: A Survivor's Tale, II: And Here My Troubles Began.* New York: Pantheon.

Stegner, W., 1976. *The Spectator Bird.* New York: Doubleday.

Yahnke, R. E., and Eastman, R. M., 1990. *Aging in Literature: A Reader's Guide.* Chicago: American Library Association.

Perspectives on Aging in Print Journalism

Maria D. Vesperi

An article published in the August 30, 1992, *New York Times* analyzed the future viability of Social Security and Medicare. After much discussion, increased payroll taxes for working people and progressive taxes on benefits for the retired were presented as the most equitable ways to shore up the system while preserving the cost-of-living increases that most benefit the low-income elderly. The article was addressed to a general audience; taxpayers of all ages were made to understand that a failure to grapple with these difficult issues would ultimately affect everyone.

Yet this otherwise exemplary approach to newspaper coverage of social welfare policy was marred by the artwork chosen to illustrate the story. Readers were drawn to the article— or warned away from it—by an accompanying photograph that was superficially unrelated but managed to narrow the context of the message quite powerfully. The cropped image displayed the legs and feet of a man, the lower part of a rubber-tipped walking cane, and the worn plank floor of a porch in sunlight. From the angle of the legs and cane it was clear that the man was seated, perhaps in a rocking chair. He was wearing cheap black dress shoes and black socks pulled high over thin legs and a swollen ankle; there was no doubt that this was an old man, idle, disabled and genteelly poor.[1] The stereotype was completed by a casual sprinkling of fallen leaves on the porch floor. Even in summer, it seems, the retired are confined to a perpetual autumn of life.

INSTITUTIONAL RESPONSES OVER TIME

Why was this photograph chosen? What does it reveal about media decision-makers and their construction of the journalist's mission to observe, record, and offer comment on old age? This article will explore such questions from the perspective of a print journalist who is also a cultural anthropologist concerned with the study of aging. The analysis will deal broadly with daily newspapers, with a focus on the content and layout of news stories rather than on advertising.

Social critics and advocates for the elderly are often unaware of the structural barriers that channel reporters, editorial writers, and advertisers into distinct, sometimes mutually contradictory arenas. The assumption that monolithic "media" are shaping the public's perception of age follows easily from this misconception about how news institutions operate. It is obvious that news text, photographs, and advertising, juxtaposed on a single page, are inseparable elements in the overall experience of reading a newspaper. However, readers who complain that the media emphasize youth and the sexual exploitation of women are often responding to advertising photos and copy, not news stories and art that require editorial judgments. (The *New York Times* photo described above would be considered news art, for instance.) It is important to be aware that the advertising and news departments of media institutions are structurally autonomous, for pragmatic, ethical, and philosophical reasons. Advertisers have been known to cancel accounts because they did not like news stories or editorials, a factor that cannot be permitted to affect news judgment. On the other hand, while news editors might well object to ageism and sexism in certain advertisements, or the promotion of certain products, the principle of free expression cuts both ways. This is why one can pick up a newspaper and find an investigative report about deception in marketing over-the-counter drugs to older people, an editorial condemning the practice and, sprinkled prominently throughout, advertisements that shamelessly exploit ageist stereotypes to sell painkillers, vitamins, and wrinkle creams.

In the mid-1970s Robert Butler's *Why Survive? Being Old in America* (1975) won a Pulitzer Prize, and a new network of social service agencies supported by the Older Americans Act was beginning to generate a demand for more local, state, and national reporting on aging. Since that time, news departments have expended varying amounts of resources on shaping their coverage to respond more sensitively to older people as subjects of stories and as readers. To date, the result of such efforts has been more of a cultural sea change than a dramatic transformation in the images of aging presented by newspapers. Valid criticisms remain, and this article will not attempt to review or debunk them. Instead, it will offer an informed view of the nascent self-reflexive process at work in the newsroom, plus a model for identifying the constructions of aging that currently shape news judgment with reference to content and intended audience. The format chosen to frame the presentation of news about age is also significant; four broad formats will be discussed here.

AGE PAGE

The "age page" represents the least sophisticated approach to aging issues. It targets older readers as an audience, beckoning to them with a distinctive format and signature logo that appear on a regular schedule, most often weekly. Age page articles are written *to* and *for* an older audience. The tone is often cute or condescending, a product of unexamined stereotypes rather than a conscious attempt to capture the attention of an older audience. The focus is on human interest and advice features, not news. Age pages devote most of their coverage to a predictable range of subjects, such as health, exercise, interpersonal relationships, and finances; these columns are generated locally or purchased from syndicates.

Age pages routinely offer features about "outstanding seniors" who can serve as upbeat role models. Older Americans, like younger ones, often establish one-sided but personally meaningful relationships with people encountered through the media (Caughey, 1984; Erikson, Erikson and Kivnick, 1986); indeed, such imaginary bonds are often encouraged. Significantly, age pages rarely feature articles that seriously challenge underlying stereotypes about late life or that probe the unresolved difficulties faced by age peers.

The age page has much in common with the "woman's" and "colored" pages that defined the mainstream media's news judgments about female and African-American readers during an earlier era. Reflecting their unequal status in the larger society, these readership groups were presumed to have highly localized and highly personalized interests. Conversely, and of greater significance from an editor's standpoint, newsworthy accomplishments by women and African Americans were not assumed to be of equal concern to other readers, who, it was further assumed, might be alienated or at best bored by such coverage. The segregated news page offered a simple solution to this dilemma, allowing the newspaper to deal with certain topics at arm's length.

Today, of course, such layouts would be rightly condemned as sexist or racist—but not ageist. In fact, the argument that young and middle-aged readers do not care about age-related issues has grown even more influential as television and periodicals expand their competition for the youth market by offering not just youth-oriented entertainment but news as well. Meanwhile, older readers are presumed to be well served by an age page, as women were once presumed satisfied with fashion and social news.

SPECIALTY SECTION

Some newspapers have expanded the age page idea into a monthly or occasional specialty section devoted to aging. Such sections are similar in content to the age page, with more room for feature stories and a wider range of advice columns. As with the age page, the specialty section includes nothing that could not appear elsewhere in the paper— nothing except age-targeted advertising, that is. The specialty section on aging gives newspapers a vehicle for vying with tabloid publications and magazines to attract residential, medical, and entertainment advertising aimed at older consumers.

THE AGING BEAT

Another approach that has grown slowly since the mid-1970s aims to present broad coverage of aging issues, with older readers as the intended primary audience. This approach requires the institution to hire or cultivate a reporter who specializes in aging, and it represents a major conceptual transition because it redefines age-related stories as news. It also requires an institutional investment in aging, just as newspapers invest in crime reporting, political coverage, foreign affairs, and dozens of other topics with designated "beats." The aging-beat reporter's assignment would include national and state-level policy issues; his or her byline would appear in various news sections as appropriate, but rarely if ever on the features pages.

One reporter with several years of experience on a high-profile aging beat for a major newspaper[2] identified his mission as providing a primarily older readership with "news they could use." A content review of his topics during a recent three-year period indicates a focus on legal and social issues, public policy, civil rights, guardianship, nursing homes, Medicare, Social Security, and political decision-making.

Overall, a commitment to such coverage communicates a media institution's recognition that aging issues—and aging people—are part of the cultural mainstream. This awareness remains tenuous in society at large, however, and this is reflected in the vulnerability of the aging beat. Relatively few newspapers designate aging as a full-time assignment; even then, it is a "luxury" beat and among the first to be put on hold in response to changing news priorities.

In the experience of the reporter cited above, who has since moved on to a different assignment, "There just wasn't much resonance around the office about what you did." Over time, he said, his travel allowance was cut back; he was also given short-term assignments to cover unrelated stories, making it difficult to keep his sources on aging current. "It's really hard to sustain a beat when people call you and you say, 'I'll get to it in a month,'" he explained. Gradually, the beat died. Significantly, however, after a two-year hiatus, his paper assigned another reporter to concentrate on aging issues.

INTEGRATED COVERAGE

A final approach to news coverage of aging issues is much more diffuse and, when properly implemented, much more indicative of long-term cultural shifts in the perception of aging and older people. The goal is to fully integrate political, medical, and social information about aging by reporting on such issues for a general readership. Medical writers and science writers are particularly adept at this approach; some of the best examples can be found in articles about medical discoveries, drug therapies, and controversies related to treatment. Rather than contribute to the stereotype that pills and sickness are the purview of the old, such articles aim to provide readers of all ages with "news they can use" for themselves or others. The *New York Times* article cited at the beginning of this paper, for instance, offers an example of political writing that invites readers of all ages to explore an issue.

Getting it right is a complex process, however. As happened with the *New York Times* piece, mistakes can involve artwork, headlines, even the placement of stories on a page. Since English-language readers are trained to scan a page from left to right, newspapers can highlight stories by placing them in the upper left corner of a section front page or signal lesser importance with a lower right corner layout. Further,

167

since a full-size newspaper is folded in half when a reader first sees it, stories that appear "below the fold" on the front cover page are pre-judged—consciously or not—as less likely to capture attention. This rough rule of thumb can be helpful in evaluating the priority a news-paper gives to aging issues over a period of time.

Such judgments are the collective product of hierarchical, compart-mentalized teamwork. The reporter's authority ends when the article is submitted; in many cases, even headline writing is a specialized job performed by someone else. In other words, each task has a separate master. Therefore, any serious effort to enhance coverage of aging issues requires ongoing internal review and a coordinated, well-articu-lated commitment to change at the level of institutional policy.

DEVELOPING SELF-REFLEXIVITY

In her introduction to *Aging and Its Discontents,* Kathleen Woodward (1991) writes:

> News stories typically begin with the name of the person followed by his or her age. We know the precise ages of our politicians and of politi-cians around the world, of celebrities, of the people who are getting married in our home towns, of the people who are arrested, and of the people who have died. As my colleague Patricia Mellencamp has point-ed out, in a news story or a gossip item the age of the person in ques-tion is often the very piece of information for which the story exists. The deep structure of the story is: name and age (p. 5).

Woodward later pinpoints examples of how tabloid journalists delight in revealing the chronological ages of public figures (pp. 161–62). Tabloid journalism is hardly the industry standard, however. While it is true that name and age remain elements of "deep structure" in many media pieces, leading news organizations have been working to bring the use of age to surface consciousness, making it available for self-reflexive examination. Returning again to the historical parallels with news coverage of women and African Americans, women were once routinely identified as wives and mothers, even when this information had nothing to do with the story. African Americans were systematical-ly identified by race; white Americans almost never were.

This excerpt from the *St. Petersburg Times* style book (Times Publishing Company, 1992) entry on women reflects significant change: "Copy should not gratuitously mention family relationships where there is no relevance to the subject....Use the same standards for men and women in deciding whether to include specific mention of personal appearance or marital and family situation" (p. 119).

Similarly, an entry on race identification spells out these distinctions: "Race often is irrelevant to a story....In crime stories, where descriptions of suspects occur, race becomes important....We are long past the days in which the lack of racial identification was understood to mean white" (p. 455). Relevance is the rule of thumb here; even in the case of crime suspects, race is not usually mentioned unless the person is actively sought by police.

There is no equivalent guideline for including or excluding the age of a subject, although writers are cautioned that the term elderly should be used "carefully and sparingly," and that it is more appropriately used to describe a group, as in "concern for the elderly, a home for the elderly," than an individual (p. 97). This does not mean, however, that age remains an unexamined aspect of deep structure. The *Times* has provided institutional support for specialized reporting on aging since the mid-1970s, resulting in a broad variety of investigative series, columns and beats, a specialty section, and a notable degree of self-reflexive attention to age stereotyping in everyday reporting. The following example shows the process at work:

During the campaign for a primary election, associates and observers of a prominent incumbent made known their opinion that he was no longer competent to perform his job. Based on the results of background research, a questionnaire, and a personal interview with the office holder, the newspaper decided to recommend a new candidate for the post. In a first draft, the writer charged with crafting the recommendation explained it this way: "Mr.————, 86, the tax collector for the past 32 years, is simply no longer prepared to devote his full attention to the job. He originally admitted that, telling people he would not seek re-election because he needed to spend time with his wife, who is recovering from illness."

The mention of how long a candidate has held office is standard in political recommendations. At this newspaper, at least, the mention of age is not. Would the inclusion of this particular incumbent's age promote a stereotype, inviting readers to conclude that he might be senile? After consulting with colleagues, the writer omitted the reference to age, a change that in no way diminished the clarity of the message. While the presence of stereotypes is all too obvious in print, the significance of their absence is more fully understood when considered as the result of a gradual change in professional practices.

CONCLUSION

Daily newspapers exist at a complex intersection of culture and community that must be continuously renegotiated. Far from the routinized maintenance of "garbage in, garbage out" that some critics envision, the presentation of news is a highly self-conscious project. News reporting, by definition, is as endless and inconclusive as the daily reality it presumes to convey. Its success is measured by the degree to which it provides readers with a credible accounting, a task that cannot be accomplished without attention to ongoing shifts in the range of information conveyed by significant cultural symbols.

Notes

1. *The Gray Panther Media Guide* (1983, p. 19) poses this question with regard to bias in illustrations: "Are the older people illustrated without stereotypic props such as canes, hearing aids, sagging clothes, rocking chairs?" All but the hearing aid are presented or suggested by the *New York Times* photograph. Listed in the *Media Guide* as signals of ageism in children's books, such cultural markers are at least equally prevalent in adult reading matter.

2. The names of reporters and their employers have been omitted to permit a more candid discussion.

References

Butler, R., 1975. *Why Survive? Being Old in America.* New York: Harper & Row.

Caughey, J., 1984. *Imaginary Social Worlds: A Cultural Approach.* Lincoln, Neb.: University of Nebraska Press.

Erikson, E., Erikson, J. and Kivnick, H., 1986. *Vital Involvement in Old Age.* New York: W. W. Norton.

Gray Panther Media Watch, 1983. *Gray Panther Media Guide.* New York: Gray Panther Media Watch Task Force.

New York Times, 1992. "Payments to the Retired Loom Even Larger," 30 August.

Times Publishing Company, 1992. Times Style. St. Petersburg, Fla.

Woodward, K., 1991. *Aging and Its Discontents: Freud and Other Fictions.* Bloomington, Ind.: Indiana University Press.

Verbal Imagery of Aging in the News Magazines

Leonard Cirillo

I n contrast to ordinary language about aging, which often masks our perceptions behind conventional words, metaphors and other figures of speech are more likely to reveal the way a speaker or writer actually views a topic. Insofar as we think about aging and the aged with a body of convenient images (Gubrium, 1973), a careful examination of the verbal imagery we usually take for granted can make us aware of the accuracy of our vision and may help us to expand our perspective on what is possible and desirable for the aged.

The news magazines—*Newsweek, Time, U.S. News & World Report*—provide a good territory for exploration. They use figures of speech more conspicuously than more formal or technical writing does, and their wide circulation suggests that these words and phrases both influence and reflect popular opinion.

Newsweek magazine inaugurated a new section on aging (Begley, Hager, and Murr, 1990) with many rhetorical tricks. In discussing a biological hypothesis about some physical changes of aging, the article explains that certain metabolic products turn "proteins rusty" (p. 45). Here "rusty," conventionally pertaining to the way exposed metals degrade, is metaphorically applied to proteins. Because the conceptions any term expresses belong to fields of related ideas (Kittay, 1987; Ullmann, 1962; Werner and Kaplan, 1963), there may be a gang of metaphors related to "rusty" waiting in the shadows.

One field to which *rusty* belongs includes terms that play roles analogous to rusty in other contexts: *corrupted, eroded, deteriorated, rotten, stale,* and so on. These connote the degradation over time of nonhuman objects. The *Newsweek* sentence just mentioned invokes another of these analogues by asserting that the same process turns "lipids rancid." *Rancid* is to fats as *rusty* is to metals.

These terms indicate that an existing system of meanings is being exploited metaphorically to organize the topic conceptually. A certain *perspective* (to use a metaphor from spatial vision) is being taken on the topic, which is now viewed through the screen provided by the borrowed language (Black, 1962; Burke, 1945, 1954, 1966). Organizing a topic according to a perspective originating elsewhere is one of the prominent functions of metaphors (Crider and Cirillo, 1991).

"Rusty" and "rancid" appear in *Newsweek's* exposition of the "wear and tear" theory of aging (Begley, Hager and Murr, 1990, p. 44), the brief introduction to which ends, "This damage accumulates until the organism falls apart, like an old jalopy" (p. 45). This comparison (a simile) is echoed in a discussion of the supposedly different "planned obsolescence" (p. 45) theory of aging: "The immune system is equally notorious for falling apart like a dishwasher past its warranty" (p. 47).

Time magazine (DeWitt, 1990), too, speaks of "planned obsolescence," claiming that it makes evolutionary sense—"Once procreation is over, human bodies may as well be disposable goods, biologically speaking"—and reports on the search for the mechanisms that make human cells "wear out" (p. 86).

U.S. News & World Report, in an article entitled "Refurbishing the Body" (Brownlee, 1990), implicitly compares the human body to a machine like an automobile that can be kept going by using "replacement parts" or "spare parts" (p. 76). Sites for replacement are indicated on a graphic of the body. An accompanying table giving "a partial list of the nearly five dozen artificial body parts now available" is entitled "the body shop" (p. 76), and another inset is dubbed, "parts of the future" (p. 77).

The body as machine may have been a fresh metaphor in Renaissance science, but the aging body as a machine wearing out and breaking down has been widespread for so long that it may sometimes lose its metaphorical status and be experienced as indubitable "fact" instead of a conceptual viewpoint (Berggren, 1962; Turbayne, 1962).

The inaugural *Newsweek* section goes beyond metaphorically equating the aging body with a deteriorating machine. Capitalizing on *rust's* belonging to another semantic field when educated people think technically, the article explicitly compares cells that are exposed to "oxidative molecules" (Begley, Hager and Murr, 1990, p. 46) with metals that are exposed to oxygen, in a paragraph that begins, "As we age, we also rust" (p. 45).

With this sentence, the article reduces the whole person to the person's bodily constituents, so that the metaphor *rust* is now predicated of "we." This reduction of person to body is implicit throughout the *Newsweek* section. Although headed "Society" and subheaded "Aging," the section is entirely devoted to the body. Even the graphics picturing individuals at various ages are accompanied by boxes that quantify maximum heart rate, lung capacity, muscle strength, kidney function—and nothing else.

The equation of person and body works both ways. Person properties are transferred to bodily constituents, resulting in some zany personifications. Citing research on people with Werner's syndrome, *Newsweek* comments, "Even their cells seem old: whereas normal cells have enough oomph to divide 50 or so times in a lab dish, those from Werner's patients divide only 10 or 20 times" (pp. 46–47). Later, a possible effect of the stress-induced release of glucocorticoids is described: "Too much hormonal stimulation, like too many screaming grandchildren, seems to make the hippocampus gray before its time" (p. 48).

This entire sequence of verbal imagery exemplifies a bad habit of pen and mind. The whole person is figuratively reduced to the bodily, and the bodily is metaphorically understood on the model of other material things, often machines. The whole aging person is thought of as a corroding, disintegrating machine.

If this were the only verbal imagery used to characterize aging, it would be a "metaphor we live by" (Lakoff and Johnson, 1980), that is, it would be so taken for granted as to be mistaken for reality. Although the imagery of machines and other artifacts wearing out is pervasive, the presence of other metaphors (Kenyon, Birren and Schroots, 1991) means that we are not prisoners of a single perspective. *Newsweek* itself contains other imagery, even mythology. Indeed, the article is entitled, "The Search for the Fountain of Youth," mentions Ponce de Leon having discovered gold in Puerto Rico, even talks of his "golden years," and intimates that "lab-coat conquistadors" are about to find the true fountain of youth, whose "springs" are "lurking" in the "precincts" of our cells and genes (Begley, Hager and Murr, 1990, p. 44).

Many isolated figures decorate the article. In discussing the "search for the underlying causes of aging," the article states, "One culprit may be glucose...which makes proteins in and between our cells stick together like gummy linguine" (p. 45). It goes on to note that "when they stick together they can...clog arteries, gum up kidney function..." and that an experimental drug may "act like flypaper," causing proteins to "stick to it rather than to one another" (p. 45). Other relatively isolated verbal images are used for the same topic, the body's microphages that "dispose of" cross-linked proteins being introduced as a "posse of cross-link scavengers" (p. 45).

Other figures occur locally for other topics without being related to the imagery just mentioned. Certain forms of oxygen and free radicals in the body are called "promiscuous" because they "react with anything that comes by" (p. 45). But the promiscuity imagery stops there and is unrelated to pasta or posses. So these images are provincial in their aspirations, composing no totalistic perspective but serving to economically make their topics concrete, familiar, and vivid (Ortony, 1975).

Although systems of verbal imagery like the worn-out machine are active in our discourse about aging, none seems to monopolize our vision. Just as stereotypic beliefs about aging (Butler, 1969) are composed of a variety of conceptual prototypes rather than a single negative stereotype (Crockett and Hummert, 1987; Hummert, 1990; Schmidt and Boland, 1986), our images of age contain diverse potentialities. Imagery that ridicules the aged as worn out and glorifies youth can be turned about with counterimagery, as in this proverb from Barbados: "The new broom sweeps cleaner, but the old broom knows the corners."

References

Begley, S., Hager, M., and Murr, A., 1990. "The Search for the Fountain of Youth." *Newsweek,* 5 March: 44–48.

Berggren, D., 1962. "The Use and Abuse of Metaphor, I and II." *The Review of Metaphysics* 16(2,3): 237–58, 450–72.

Black, M., 1962. *Models and Metaphors.* Ithaca, N.Y.: Cornell University Press.

Brownlee, S., 1990. "Refurbishing the Body." *U.S. News & World Report,* 12 November: 76–78.

Burke, K., 1945. *A Grammar of Motives.* New York: Prentice-Hall.

Burke, K., 1954. *Permanence and Change,* 2d rev. ed. Los Altos, Calif.: Hermes.

Burke, K., 1966. *Language as Symbolic Action: Essays on Life, Literature, and Method.* Berkeley, Calif.: University of California Press.

Butler, R. N., 1969. "Age-ism: Another Form of Bigotry." Gerontologist 9(4): 243–46.

Crider, C., and Cirillo, L., 1991. "Systems of Interpretation and the Function of Metaphor." *Journal for the Theory of Social Behavior* 21(2): 171–95.

Crockett, W. H., and Hummert, M. L., 1987. "Perceptions of Aging and the Elderly." In K. W. Schaie, ed., *Annual Review of Gerontology and Geriatrics* 7: 217–41.

DeWitt, P. E., 1990. "You Should Live So Long." *Time,* 12 November: 86.

Gubrium, J. F., 1973. *The Myth of the Golden Years.* Springfield, Ill.: Charles C. Thomas.

Hummert, M. L., 1990. "Multiple Stereotypes of Elderly and Young Adults: A Comparison of Structure and Evaluations." *Psychology and Aging* 5(2): 182–93.

Kenyon, G. M., Birren, J. F. and Schroots, J. J. F., eds., 1991. *Metaphors of Aging in Science and the Humanities.* New York: Springer Publishing Co.

Kittay, E. F., 1987. *Metaphor: Its Cognitive Force and Linguistic Structure.* New York: Oxford University Press.

Lakoff, G., and Johnson, M., 1980. *Metaphors We Live By.* Chicago: University of Chicago Press.

Ortony, A., 1975. "Why Metaphors Are Necessary and Not Just Nice." *Educational Theory* 25: 45–53.

Schmidt, D. F., and Boland, S. M., 1986. "Structure of Perceptions of Older Adults: Evidence for Multiple StereoTypes." *Psychology and Aging* 1(3): 255–60.

Turbayne, C. M., 1962. *The Myth of Metaphor.* New Haven, Conn.: Yale University Press.

Ullmann, S., 1962. *Semantics: An Introduction to the Science of Meaning.* New York: Barnes & Noble.

Werner, H., and Kaplan, B., 1963. *Symbol Formation.* New York: Wiley.

Index